Cambridge Elements

Cambridge Elements in International Economics
edited by
Kenneth A. Reinert
George Mason University

GLOBAL VALUE CHAINS IN SOUTHEAST ASIA

Upalat Korwatanasakul
Waseda University and Shibaura Institute of Technology

Adiasri Putri Purbantina
University of Pembangunan Nasional "Veteran" Jawa Timur

Tran Thi Hue
Kobe Women's University

Ha Thi Thanh Doan
Economic Research Institute for ASEAN and East Asia

CAMBRIDGE
UNIVERSITY PRESS

CAMBRIDGE
UNIVERSITY PRESS

Shaftesbury Road, Cambridge CB2 8EA, United Kingdom

One Liberty Plaza, 20th Floor, New York, NY 10006, USA

477 Williamstown Road, Port Melbourne, VIC 3207, Australia

314–321, 3rd Floor, Plot 3, Splendor Forum, Jasola District Centre,
New Delhi – 110025, India

Cambridge University Press is part of Cambridge University Press & Assessment,
a department of the University of Cambridge.

We share the University's mission to contribute to society through the pursuit of
education, learning and research at the highest international levels of excellence.

www.cambridge.org
Information on this title: www.cambridge.org/9781009673860

DOI: 10.1017/9781009673839

When citing this work, please include a reference to the DOI 10.1017/9781009673839

First published 2026

A catalogue record for this publication is available from the British Library

*A Cataloging-in-Publication data record for this Element is available from
the Library of Congress*

ISBN 978-1-009-67386-0 Hardback
ISBN 978-1-009-67385-3 Paperback
ISSN 2753-9326 (online)
ISSN 2753-9318 (print)

Global Value Chains in Southeast Asia

Cambridge Elements in International Economics

DOI: 10.1017/9781009673839
First published online: July 2026

Upalat Korwatanasakul
Waseda University and Shibaura Institute of Technology

Adiasri Putri Purbantina
University of Pembangunan Nasional "Veteran" Jawa Timur

Tran Thi Hue
Kobe Women's University

Ha Thi Thanh Doan
Economic Research Institute for ASEAN and East Asia

Author for correspondence: Upalat Korwatanasakul,
upalat@shibaura-it.ac.jp

Abstract: This Element explores the developmental implications of Southeast Asia's participation in global value chains (GVCs), focusing on the coffee, textile and clothing, and automotive sectors. While GVC integration has supported industrialisation, exports, and employment, the benefits are not guaranteed. Southeast Asian countries, except for a few cases, remain confined to low-value-added activities, with limited innovation, weak support for small and medium-sized enterprises (SMEs), and persistent inequality. Sectoral case studies reveal barriers to upgrading: smallholder coffee farmers face institutional and coordination challenges; textile and clothing producers in Cambodia and Myanmar are stuck in low-skill roles; and domestic automotive firms struggle to move beyond assembly. The Element calls for a shift from passive participation to active upgrading through stronger innovation systems, SME support, social and environmental standards, and deeper regional cooperation. It concludes that GVCs can promote inclusive and sustainable growth—but only when embedded in deliberate national and regional strategies.

Keywords: global value chain, inclusive development, industrial upgrading, sectoral case studies, Southeast Asia

ISBNs: 9781009673860 (HB), 9781009673853 (PB), 9781009673839 (OC)
ISSNs: 2753-9326 (online), 2753-9318 (print)

Contents

expansion, knowledge acquisition, and innovation (e.g., APEC Study Center, 2017; Korwatanasakul & Paweenawat, 2021; OECD, 2008).

At the labour market level – one key advantage of GVC participation is its contribution to job creation, as GVC-oriented investment can increase employment opportunities (Korwatanasakul et al., 2022). Although trends show a growing demand for medium- and high-skilled labour, GVCs in developing countries often still generate jobs for low-skilled workers, especially in export-driven industries. This expansion can raise domestic employment levels and integrate local workers into global production networks.

Another potential benefit lies in skills development and working conditions. While the evidence remains mixed, GVC participation may facilitate skill upgrading and promote better working environments by exposing workers to international standards and practices. This effect tends to be more pronounced in developed economies, but it could also emerge in developing countries, particularly when combined with targeted investment in training and technology transfer. For instance, Hue and Korwatanasakul (2023) support the positive impact of GVC participation on labour productivity. Evidence suggests that forward participation in GVCs – primarily through exports – is positively associated with productivity improvements, higher wages, and improved employment outcomes.

The wage and income effects of GVC participation are complex. Still, some studies suggest it can lead to higher wages, particularly for workers in exporting sectors or industries with strong backward linkages (Korwatanasakul et al., 2022). Evidence shows that GVC integration is associated with higher wages, primarily due to increased labour demand from growing export sectors and offshoring (Korwatanasakul et al., 2022). GVC engagement has been associated with reduced wage inequality in certain instances, especially when lower-skilled workers gain access to training and technology that enhance their productivity. For example, forward GVC participation tends to be more inclusive, benefiting workers across genders, skill levels, and regions. These linkages contribute to more equitable wage distribution and employment gains (Korwatanasakul et al., 2022). However, these benefits are not uniform and may depend on the type of GVC activities and the demographic composition of the workforce. Backward GVC participation, involving imported foreign inputs, also raises wages but more selectively – particularly among male workers, rural populations, and low-skilled labour (Korwatanasakul et al., 2022). This is most evident in manufacturing industries, where foreign investment creates jobs and enhances pay. However, in non-manufacturing sectors or regions with limited absorptive capacity, backward participation may yield mixed or even adverse effects (Korwatanasakul et al., 2022).

Finally, GVCs may enhance labour market inclusion by expanding opportunities for groups that are typically underrepresented, such as youth, rural residents, women, and low-skilled workers. In settings where low-skilled labour is in demand, GVC participation can improve access to employment for these groups, contributing to broader economic inclusion. Despite ongoing concerns about persistent gender wage gaps and unequal working conditions, the evidence shows that GVCs have the potential to support more inclusive labour market outcomes if supported by appropriate policy frameworks.

1.2 Risks of GVC Participation

While participation in GVCs can drive early industrialisation and export growth, it carries significant risks, particularly for developing economies. The benefits of backward participation – through the import of foreign inputs – are nuanced. While such participation can offer technological gains, heavy reliance on foreign inputs without domestic upgrading may lead to adverse outcomes (Korwatanasakul, 2023a). This partially contradicts the learning-to-learn hypothesis and highlights the risks of remaining in low-value-added positions within GVCs.

One major concern is the middle-income technology trap – a situation in which countries remain locked into low-value-added segments of production, such as labour-intensive assembly, without transitioning to more knowledge- and technology-intensive activities (Korwatanasakul, 2023a). This technological stagnation can ultimately contribute to the broader middle-income trap, where countries experience slow growth and fail to reach high-income status (Goto, 2011; Korwatanasakul, 2023a; Lee et al., 2021).

Second, developing countries often experience passive and peripheral participation in GVCs, with local firms playing minor roles in lower tiers of production networks and remaining dependent on foreign technology, capital, and managerial expertise (Korwatanasakul, 2023a, 2023b; Le, 2015; Truong, 2008). This limits their capacity to develop domestic innovation systems or climb the value chain. In many cases, firms operate as contract manufacturers or assemblers with little control over branding, design, or strategic decision-making. As a result, even as trade volumes grow, the domestic developmental benefits remain limited.

Third, a lack of effective knowledge and technology transfer poses a significant challenge. In modular production systems, such as those in the automotive and electronics industries, lead firms often exert control over innovation and limit interactions with local suppliers (Korwatanasakul, 2019, 2023a, 2023b; Korwatanasakul & Intarakumnerd, 2020, 2021; Le, 2015). This isolation prevents domestic firms from accessing high-value activities, such as design and research and development (R&D) hindering their prospects for upgrading. In many ASEAN economies, domestic suppliers are stuck producing low-tech components without meaningful exposure to frontier technologies. The asymmetry in knowledge flows reinforces dependency and leaves local firms ill-prepared to move beyond low-cost roles.

Fourth, over-reliance on FVA inputs creates additional vulnerabilities as heavy dependence on imported intermediates undermines domestic value creation and exposes industries to global supply chain disruptions (Hill et al., 2020; Intarakumnerd & Korwatansakul, 2020). This structural dependence weakens industrial resilience and limits the sustainability of GVC-led growth. For instance, disruptions in upstream suppliers – whether due to trade tensions or natural disasters – can cascade through production networks, halting output in downstream economies. Moreover, this reliance on foreign inputs limits opportunities to nurture domestic supplier ecosystems.

Fifth, weak institutional frameworks exacerbate these challenges (Korwatanasakul, 2019, 2023a; Korwatanasakul & Purbantina, 2021; Thanh & Ha, 2004). Developing economies lack adequate R&D investment, science and technology infrastructure, and innovation support systems. Without coordinated policies to strengthen domestic capabilities, countries struggle to harness GVC participation for long-term development. In many cases, fragmented governance and inconsistent policy implementation prevent effective industrial upgrading. Stronger institutions are needed to coordinate stakeholder interests, mobilise resources, and provide the long-term vision necessary for innovation-led growth.

Sixth, these structural issues can lead to premature deindustrialisation – a scenario in which countries lose their manufacturing base before reaching high-income status (Korwatanasakul, 2023a). Rising wages and eroding comparative advantage in low-cost labour, combined with weak upgrading capacity, can stall economic transformation. As global production shifts towards capital-intensive and digital technologies, countries that fail to climb the value chain may find themselves priced out of manufacturing altogether. This raises concerns about employment, income distribution, and the viability of industrial policy.

Lastly, GVCs can reinforce structural dependencies and unequal bargaining power dynamics. Local firms, particularly SMEs, often have limited bargaining power when dealing with dominant global lead firms (Hatsukano & Tanaka, 2014; Korwatanasakul & Paweenawat, 2021). This imbalance restricts their influence over pricing, quality standards, and innovation, leading to an uneven distribution of GVC benefits that disproportionately favours multinational corporations (MNCs). Power asymmetries also make it difficult for local firms to negotiate fair contracts or protect their intellectual property. Unless mechanisms are introduced to enhance the voice and capabilities of domestic suppliers, GVC participation may entrench, rather than alleviate, existing inequalities.

1.3 About the Element

To examine the sector-specific dynamics and policy implications of GVC participation, this Element focuses on three strategically important industries in the ASEAN region: agribusiness (coffee), textiles and clothing, and automobiles. These sectors are central to ASEAN's industrial structure, are deeply integrated into global and RVCs, and are highly exposed to external shocks, such as the United States (US) reciprocal tariffs. Their development has been shaped by extensive engagement with transnational corporations through both FDI and non-equity modes of operation, generating dense cross-border ownership and production linkages that have also supported regional integration. Given their economic and strategic importance, together with well-developed GVC and RVC dynamics, these industries provide a suitable basis for analysing common patterns, sectoral differences, and policy challenges related to upgrading and value capture in the ASEAN context. Each case study highlights unique developmental opportunities and structural challenges in integrating into and upgrading within GVCs.

Across these sectors, the Element is guided by four overarching research questions:

(1) How are ASEAN economies positioned within GVCs and RVCs, and what structural factors determine their roles across different industries?
(2) Why does deep participation in GVCs often fail to translate into higher DVA and inclusive development outcomes in ASEAN?
(3) What constraints limit upgrading and value capture by local firms and SMEs within GVCs, and how do these constraints differ across countries and sectors?
(4) What policy and institutional frameworks are most effective in leveraging GVC and RVC participation to promote resilient, inclusive, and sustainable sectoral development in ASEAN?

Agribusiness (coffee) – This section explores the structure, dynamics, and implications of the coffee value chain in Southeast Asia, situating the discussion within the broader context of GVCs. While much of the GVC literature focuses on industrial sectors, this section focuses on high-value agricultural products – specifically coffee – and their developmental significance for ASEAN economies. The analysis underscores how coffee-producing countries, such as Indonesia, the Lao PDR, Thailand, and Vietnam, participate in the global coffee trade, with each exhibiting distinct production models, export patterns, and levels of value chain integration. Through a comparative and country-specific lens, the section reveals that while ASEAN countries are major green coffee exporters, their roles are primarily confined to upstream activities, leaving value-added processes, such as roasting and branding, to foreign firms.

The section adopts GVC participation metrics, such as DVA and FVA, to assess each country's position within international production networks. It also highlights smallholder farmers' structural constraints, particularly in Indonesia, where power asymmetries and midstream bottlenecks (the hidden middle) limit their opportunities for upgrading. While specialty coffee offers potential for rural development and branding-driven value capture, policy coordination, infrastructure, and equitable governance remain critical challenges. Drawing on empirical evidence, interviews, and trade data, this section contributes to a deeper understanding of Southeast Asia's agricultural GVCs and offers insights for designing more inclusive and development-oriented value chain strategies.

Textiles and Clothing – This section examines the evolution, dynamics, and challenges of ASEAN's participation in the textile and clothing (T&C) GVCs, focusing on Cambodia, Myanmar, and Vietnam. ASEAN has emerged as a key region in labour-intensive manufacturing, with the T&C sector playing a crucial role in driving export growth, creating employment, and fostering industrial development. Drawing on backward and forward linkage data, firm-level trends, FDI inflows, labour costs, and regional production networks, the section maps ASEAN's deepening integration into GVCs while highlighting the persistence of structural constraints. While countries like Vietnam have successfully attracted FDI and pursued partial upgrading, Cambodia and Myanmar remain trapped in low-value assembly roles, characterised by import dependency, weak domestic linkages, and limited innovation. The analysis identifies key challenges facing the sector, including limited vertical integration, inadequate capabilities among SMEs, rising labour costs without corresponding productivity gains, and underinvestment in sustainability. Industrial policies in the three countries reveal divergent trajectories in balancing GVC integration with sustainable growth, with Vietnam taking a more coordinated approach. The section concludes with targeted policy recommendations to enhance vertical integration, support SME innovation, advance social upgrading, and promote circular economy practices. These insights contribute to broader debates on inclusive industrial development and resilient GVC participation in the ASEAN region.

Automobiles – The automotive sector plays a pivotal role in the economies of ASEAN member states, contributing significantly to regional GDP and employment. ASEAN has established itself as a key production hub for a range of vehicles, including cars, motorcycles, and trucks, as well as their components. Despite the industry's complexity and multi-tiered structure, production processes have been globally fragmented and integrated into regional and international value chains through GVCs. However, the sector in ASEAN is often characterised by lower value addition and limited multiplier effects. The degree of value added in exports varies among countries, influenced by each nation's specific position within the automotive value chain. Over time, GVC participation has slightly declined, attributed to increased local value creation. Conversely, participation in RVCs has increased gradually. Both GVC and RVC engagements are characterised by strong backward linkages, indicating high FVA, and a steady increase in forward linkages, reflecting the growing domestic value incorporated into other countries' exports.

ASEAN's prominence in the global automotive landscape, often referred to as 'Factory Asia', has grown considerably. Each member country has developed specialised niches within the automotive value chain, establishing a solid foundation for potential industrial upgrading. ASEAN requires a comprehensive policy framework to further enhance the region's role in the global automotive value chain. Such a framework should prioritise the integration and development of domestic enterprises, particularly SMEs. Emphasis should be placed on capacity building through research and development and technological innovation, enabling these firms to move up the value chain. Additionally, fostering regional cooperation – such as creating a shared database of parts suppliers and establishing regional certification systems for human resources – will be crucial for sustained growth and competitiveness.

This introductory section has outlined the conceptual and empirical significance of GVCs in shaping ASEAN's economic development. While GVC participation brings clear opportunities for productivity gains, wage growth, and industrial upgrading, it also presents risks – particularly for economies that remain in low-value-added roles without effective upgrading strategies. The following sections build on this foundation by examining sector-specific dynamics in coffee, textiles and clothing, and automotive industries. These case studies highlight the diversity of ASEAN's GVC engagement and offer valuable insights into how policies, firm capabilities, and global trends interact to shape inclusive and resilient development pathways.

2 Agrobusiness (Coffee) Value Chain

2.1 Introduction

Southeast Asia has become a key hub for agricultural and agrifood trade as GVCs reshape international trade, enabling goods to cross borders multiple times, from raw materials to finished products. This section examines the region's interconnectedness with global economies, particularly China and the US, and the dynamics shaping ASEAN agriculture, which remains vital for employment and income generation. The evolving agricultural landscape, including the rise of food delivery platforms and local coffee shops, highlights the challenges and opportunities of GVC participation.

Through the coffee value chain, this section examines the agribusiness industry's role in regional economies, analysing production and trade trends in Indonesia, the Lao PDR, Thailand, and Vietnam, where coffee plays a significant economic role and exhibits a distinct industry structure. Coffee, one of the world's most traded agricultural commodities, is integral to the global agribusiness industry, yet its statistics remain fragmented. Agriculture and forestry value-added statistics capture coffee only at the farm level, while manufacturing data subsume it within broader beverage categories. These datasets therefore offer a broad structural view in which coffee originates as agriculture in producing countries and culminates as manufacturing in consuming countries (Section 2.2).

Endowment factors and geographical advantages shape Southeast Asia's agricultural strength. For resource-abundant countries, agriculture remains a core economic sector, significantly impacting exports, GDP, and SMEs (Figure 1 and Table 1). Additionally, agriculture plays a crucial role in employment, particularly in middle-income Southeast Asian countries (Table 2). While discussions on GVCs in catching-up economies often focus on middle- to high-end manufacturing sectors (e.g., electronics and automotive), development in Southeast Asia remains anchored in agriculture and agro-based industries, such as food and beverage processing, making their GVC participation centred on agricultural exports and their role as global suppliers (Figure 2).

Studies on GVCs indicate that participation in GVCs benefits local economic actors in developing countries by enabling them to access the international market, enhance their technological capabilities, and gradually transition to higher-value activities (OECD, 2015). In high-value agricultural products such as coffee, participation can improve productivity and foster economic growth. Therefore, upgrading within GVCs (i.e., moving from upstream, low-value activities to downstream, higher-value activities such as processing and branding) is critical and challenging for local actors

Table 1 ASEAN exports of agricultural products (2013 & 2022) (in million $).

HS Code	Description	2013	2022	Average Annual Growth 2013–2022
01	Animals; live	434.6	620	10.90%
02	Meat and edible meat offal	658.7	1,656.40	11.50%
03	Fish and crustaceans, molluscs and other aquatic invertebrates	12,117.90	15,712.40	3.30%
04	Dairy produce; birds' eggs; natural honey; edible products of animal origin, not elsewhere specified or included	1,648.30	2,320.00	4.20%
05	Animal-originated products; not elsewhere specified or included	144.6	264.8	8.90%
06	Trees and other plants, live; bulbs, roots and the like; cut flowers and ornamental foliage	371.4	393	1.00%
07	Vegetables and certain roots and tubers; edible	3,483.30	4,993.90	5.20%
08	Fruit and nuts, edible; peel of citrus fruit or melons	5,390.10	14,519.20	12.60%
09	**Coffee, tea, mate and spices**	5,987.10	7,040.90	**2.30%**
10	Cereals	8,462.60	9,445.00	2.00%
11	Products of the milling industry; malt, starches, inulin, wheat gluten	2,367.20	3,848.80	6.00%
12	Oilseeds and oleaginous fruits; miscellaneous grains, seeds and fruit, industrial or medicinal plants; straw and fodder	1,216.50	1,398.70	2.20%
13	Lac; gums, resins and other vegetable saps and extracts	396.4	791.7	9.20%
14	Vegetable plaiting materials; vegetable products not elsewhere specified or included	159.9	706.3	18.40%
15	Animal or vegetable fats and oils and their cleavage products; prepared animal fats; animal or vegetable waxes	37,683.80	64,664.90	8.00%

Table 1 (cont.)

HS Code	Description	2013	2022	Average Annual Growth 2013–2022
16	Meat, fish or crustaceans, molluscs or other aquatic invertebrates; preparations thereof	10,690.40	12,290.30	1.70%
17	Sugars and sugar confectionery	4,656.30	5,410.00	3.50%
18	Cocoa and cocoa preparations	3,102.00	4,057.10	3.30%
19	Preparations of cereals, flour, starch or milk; pastrycooks' products	5,181.40	7,397.90	4.20%
20	Preparations of vegetables, fruit, nuts or other parts of plants	3,252.30	5,397.20	6.00%
21	Miscellaneous edible preparations	5,544.00	14,618.00	12.20%
22	Beverages, spirits and vinegar	5,460.00	6,227.40	1.80%
23	Food industries, residues and wastes thereof; prepared animal fodder	3,571.50	8,294.80	10.50%
24	Tobacco and manufactured tobacco substitutes	2,985.90	2,973.20	0.40%
–	**TOTAL**	**434.6**	**195,041.80**	**5.40%**

Source: ASEAN Secretariat (2023)

to capture greater economic benefit, especially within a GVC governance model with more complex transaction and information codifiability (see Gereffi et al., 2005; Fernandez-Stark et al., 2012). Participating in GVCs enables farmers and small agribusinesses in low- and middle-income countries to access international markets and leverage their comparative advantages. However, data scarcity in the 'hidden middle' (midstream) of agrifood value chains limits understanding of these processes (Bellemare et al., 2022). The value chain structure results in a disproportionate distribution of final consumer prices, with only 16% captured at the input and production stages (Cucagna & Goldsmith, 2018). This highlights the significance of post-harvest value chain intermediation, encompassing processing, storage, transportation, and retail, in transforming raw commodities into consumer-ready foods (Yi et al., 2021).

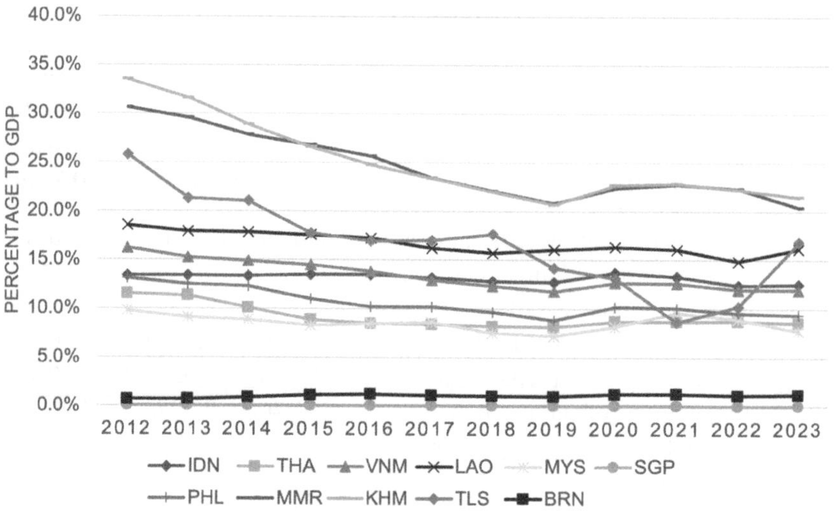

Figure 1 Agriculture, forestry, and fishing, value added: Southeast Asian countries.

Source: World Bank (2025a)

Unlike medium-high-technology manufacturing, which often follows a producer-driven governance structure, global agricultural value chains are typically buyer- or market-driven. In coffee, major brands and traders control design, marketing, and sales while outsourcing production. Suppliers compete under power asymmetries, with MNCs and downstream actors dictating pricing, standards, and market access. By 2018, large firms such as Nestlé and JAB Holding controlled nearly 38% of the global roasting market, where their profitability rested on brand power and intangible value creation (e.g., innovation, marketing, and consumer experiences). In contrast, farmers remained tied to volatile commodity markets. They lack insight into consumer markets and limited control over the final form or destination of their coffee exports, leaving them at a disadvantage in negotiations. As a consequence, studies show they gained only a fraction of the total value (BASIC, 2024; Grabs, 2017; Sachs et al., 2019, 2025).

Existing policy interventions have not fully corrected these imbalances, which originated from persistent information asymmetries within a buyer-driven structure. Studies show that in the French and German coffee markets, upstream actors captured only a fraction of total value, while downstream margins overshadow farmgate returns (Sachs et al., 2019; Sachs et al., 2025). Governments and international organisations have promoted upgrading through certifications, origin designations, and sustainability programmes (see Devaux et al., 2018; Hirpato, 2022; Suryana et al., 2023; Tampubolon

Table 2 Proportion of employment in ASEAN by economic activity.

	Agriculture, Fishery & Forestry	Manufacturing	Construct-ion	Wholesales & Retail Trade, Restaurants, & Hotels	Transportation, Storage, Information & Communication	Finance, Insurance, Real Estate & Business Services	Public Services	Others
Brunei Darussalam (2022)	1.5%	6.5%	8.9%	22.8%	5.2%	10.7%	32.2%	12.1%
Cambodia (2019)	33.1%	16.7%	10.0%	20.2%	5.0%	2.5%	5.9%	6.7%
Indonesia (2022)	28.6%	14.2%	6.3%	26.5%	5.0%	3.2%	10.1%	6.2%
The Lao PDR (2022)	57.5%	4.7%	4.9%	14.3%	2.6%	4.0%	8.9%	3.2%
Malaysia (2022)	10.0%	16.8%	7.6%	29.1%	6.2%	11.1%	14.9%	4.3%
Myanmar (2019)	48.9%	10.4%	5.6%	20.0%	5.8%	2.1%	3.3%	3.9%
The Philippines (2022)	23.1%	8.0%	9.3%	26.0%	8.0%	7.3%	10.6%	7.7%
Singapore (2022)	N/A	9.6%	4.2%	20.4%	14.5%	26.1%	24.4%	0.9%
Thailand (2022)	30.4%	16.0%	5.6%	24.6%	4.3%	4.9%	9.6%	4.6%
Vietnam (2022)	27.5%	23.3%	9.2%	20.9%	4.4%	1.7%	8.9%	4.2%

Source: ASEAN Secretariat (2023)

Notes: (a) Data for Singapore refer to residents only; (b) Data for Agriculture, Fishery & Forestry of Singapore are subsumed under 'Others (Mining & Quarrying, Electricity, Gas & Water, Unknown)'; N/A = not available.

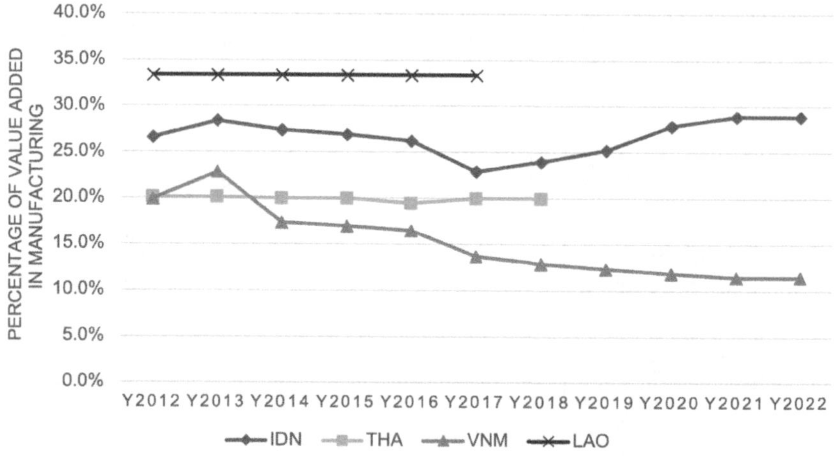

Figure 2 Food, beverages, and tobacco (% of value added in manufacturing): Selected ASEAN countries (2012–2022).

Source: World Bank (2025c)

et al., 2023). However, downstream actors often use sustainability claims only to justify higher retail prices without redistributing value to farmers, even though they face greater exposure to sustainability issues than upstream actors. The International Coffee Organization (ICO) (2024) highlights that smallholders remain mostly affected by climate change, resource competition, and declining soil fertility, while downstream actors capture new opportunities through circular economy initiatives and regenerative branding (ICO, 2024). A mismatch that reinforced structural inequality, which occurred because: (1) the existence of intangible value creations, such as branding and marketing, that become the primary source of profitability; and (2) the presence of intermediary actors, also known as the 'hidden middle', which controls midstream processes between farmers and roasters.

2.2 Coffee Value Chain in Southeast Asia

Coffee, especially specialty coffee, is a key high-value agricultural commodity. The global coffee industry connects growers to consumers and drives economic stability in Indonesia, the Lao PDR, Thailand, and Vietnam, supporting export revenues and rural livelihoods. These nations have distinct policy approaches shaped by socio-economic contexts and market dynamics. However, their focus on upstream activities (i.e., cultivation and initial processing) limits access to high-value segments, such as roasting and branding, which remain under the control of external players. This uneven distribution of value restricts economic benefits and underscores the need for strategic interventions to strengthen participation in downstream activities.

The coffee value chain for Robusta and Arabica includes various stages that transform green coffee beans into final products. Green coffee beans are transported from their origins, primarily in developing countries located in the coffee belt region, including Southeast Asian countries, to be processed and roasted in specialised roasting facilities. Within the global coffee value chain led by large multinational coffee brands (Table 3), most green coffee beans are transported from developing to developed countries as the latter adds the most value (Daly et al., 2018; ITC, 2021). It is also important to note that most roasting machine manufacturers are based in Europe (Tables 4 and 5).

In 2022, unroasted coffee (non-decaffeinated) was the world's 109th most traded product, with a total trade value of $29.7 billion, representing 0.13 % of global trade. The top importers were the US ($6.66 billion), Germany ($4.08 billion), Italy ($2.17 billion), Belgium ($2.14 billion), and Japan ($1.49 billion). These importing countries accounted for a significant portion of global imports, driven by their robust coffee consumption and processing industries. Recent data from 2023 indicates a slight decline in trade value to $26.5 billion, with the US ($5.4 billion), Germany ($3.06 billion), Italy ($2.14 billion), Japan ($1.38 billion), and Belgium ($1.07 billion) remaining the top importers (OEC, 2025b).

According to the ICO (2025) and the Observatory of Economic Complexity (OEC) (2025a, 2025b), three Southeast Asian countries are key players in the global coffee value chain. Vietnam is the world's largest producer of Robusta coffee, accounting for approximately 97% of its coffee production. In the 2023–2024 season, Vietnam exported approximately 1.45 million tons of coffee. The European Union (EU) is its key market (38% of its export volume). Indonesia is the second-largest coffee exporter in Southeast Asia and the world's third-largest producer of Robusta coffee. Indonesia's primary coffee export markets include Egypt, Japan, Malaysia, and the US. Although the Lao PDR's coffee export volume is significantly lower than that of Indonesia and Vietnam, coffee is the Lao PDR's third-largest agricultural export product (Figure 3). Interestingly, a significant portion of the Lao PDR's coffee exports is destined for Thailand and Vietnam. Thailand is not a significant coffee-exporting country, but several studies highlight the success story of Arabica coffee from the North and Northeast of Thailand.

Table 3 Examples of renowned multinational coffee companies.

No	Company names	Products	Country of origins & production facilities	Sourcing countries
1	Nestlé S.A. (1866)	Instant coffee (Nescafé), roasted coffee beans (Nespresso, Blue Bottle Coffee); Starbucks (licensed products)	Germany, Switzerland, United States	Brazil, Colombia, Ethiopia, Indonesia, Vietnam
2	Starbucks Corporation (1971)	Roasted coffee beans, ground coffee, and Starbucks VIA Instant Coffee.	United States	Brazil, Colombia, Ethiopia, Guatemala, Indonesia, and Vietnam
3	JDE Peet's (2015 merger of Jacobs Douwe Egberts and Peet's Coffee)	Instant coffee (Jacobs, Douwe Egberts), roasted coffee beans (Peet's Coffee, L'OR).	Netherlands	Brazil, Colombia, Ethiopia, Indonesia, and Vietnam
4	The Kraft Heinz Company	Instant coffee (Maxwell House), roasted coffee beans (Gevalia)	United States	Brazil and Colombia (Limited information available on sourcing from Southeast Asia)
5	Lavazza Group	Roasted coffee beans (Lavazza, Carte Noire, Merrild)	Italy	Brazil, Colombia, Costa Rica, Guatemala, Honduras, Indonesia, Uganda, and Vietnam

Source: Authors, based on JDE Peet (2025); Kraft Heinz (2021); Lacazza World (2022); Nestlé (2023); Starbucks (2025)

Notes: In addition, according to Euromonitor International (2024), regional coffee chains with a significant presence in Southeast Asia include Luckin Coffee and Cotti Coffee, both originating in China. However, there is limited information regarding their sourcing countries.

Table 4 Examples of renowned coffee roasting machine companies.

No	Company name	Year of establishment	Origin & manufacturing site location	Users
1	Probat	1868	Germany	Starbucks and Lavazza
2	Bühler Group	1860	Switzerland	Used by large-scale coffee producers and chains, although specific names are not mentioned on their website
3	Petroncini	1919	Italy	Used by various coffee brands especially for speciality coffee, but specific multinational chains are not listed on their website
4	Scolari Engineering	1950	Italy	Known for its industrial coffee roasting solutions
5	Leogap	1963	Brazil	They are recognised as a key supplier in the Brazilian coffee industry

Source: Authors, based on Bühler Group (2025); Leogap (2025); Petroncini (2019); Probat (2025); Scolari Engineering (2025)

2.2.1 Indonesia

Indonesia has one of the highest trade values in value-added figures in agriculture and food manufacturing, reflecting its substantial presence in global supply chains. While its international trade is significant, a large portion of its final demand is domestic, indicating robust internal consumption and industrial processing. Its reliance on foreign inputs is moderate in comparison to the other three countries, with a smaller share of ASEAN-focused trade compared to its global exports (Table 6). As of 2022, Indonesia was the second-largest coffee exporter in Southeast Asia, contributing 12.4 % to GDP. In 2021, exports reached $ 902 million, with primary destinations including Egypt, Japan, Malaysia, Spain, and the US (Table 7).

Coffee production grew between 2019 and 2021 but declined 16.5% in 2023/24 due to excessive rainfall damaging crops, causing exports to drop by 23%. Despite being a top global producer, Indonesia's yield per hectare remains lower

Table 5 Examples of renowned major espresso machine manufacturers.

No	Company names	Country of origin (year of establishment)	Global partners
1	Thermoplan AG	Switzerland (1974)	Starbucks (exclusive supplier of the Mastrena series); McCafe – McDonald's coffee chain; IKEA
2	La Marzocco	Italy (1927)	Starbucks Reserve, Blue Bottle Coffee
3	Rancilio	Italy (1927)	McCafe – McDonald's coffee chain
4	Nuova Simonelli	Italy (1936)	Used in World Barista Championships and by various specialty coffee shops
5	Eversys	Switzerland (2009)	Starbucks

Source: Authors, based on Eversys (2025); La Marzocco (2025); Rancilio Group (2024); Simonelli Group (2025); Thermoplan AG (2025)

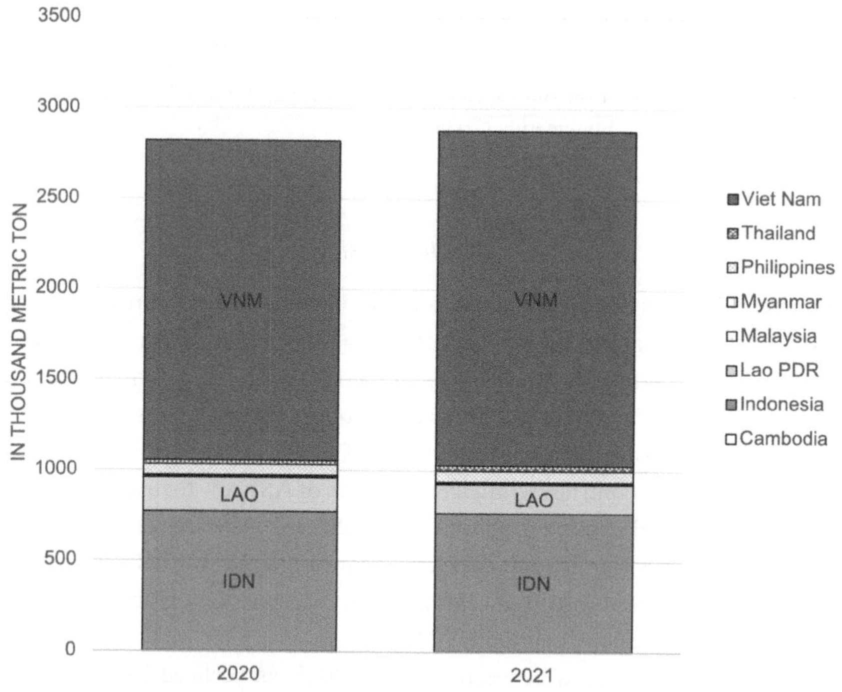

Figure 3 Production of coffee (green beans) in ASEAN (2020–2021).
Source: ASEAN Secretariat (2025)

Table 6 Indonesia's trade value added (in million $).

A. Agriculture and forestry

Value added\Year	2015	2016	2017	2018	2019	2020
DVA in gross exports: World	5,517	5,255	5,876	6,269	5,903	5,635
DVA in gross exports: ASEAN	745	587	579	746	618	662
FVA in gross exports: World	196	163	195	239	200	158
FVA in gross exports: ASEAN	N/A	N/A	N/A	N/A	N/A	N/A
DVA in foreign final demand: World	15,452	15,643	17,598	17,595	16,883	16,484
DVA in foreign final demand: ASEAN	1,524	1,488	1,586	1,758	1,692	1,700
FVA in domestic final demand: World	7,643	7,303	8,033	9,693	9,068	7,153
FVA in domestic final demand: ASEAN	1,006	1,031	1,125	1,558	1,281	785

B. Manufacture of food products, beverages and tobacco products

Value added\Year	2015	2016	2017	2018	2019	2020
DVA in gross exports: World	20,573	20,857	24,583	24,788	23,560	22,393
DVA in gross exports: ASEAN	2,309	2,411	2,680	2,972	3,033	3,084
FVA in gross exports: World	1,749	1,461	1,844	2,130	1,743	1,294
FVA in gross exports: ASEAN	N/A	N/A	N/A	N/A	N/A	N/A
DVA in foreign final demand: World	10,855	11,942	14,186	14,605	14,152	13,620
DVA in foreign final demand: ASEAN	1,057	1,221	1,393	1,558	1,633	1,636
FVA in domestic final demand: World	3,427	3,169	3,566	4,342	4,102	3,110
FVA in domestic final demand: ASEAN	723	761	820	1,143	956	542

Source: Authors, based on OECD (2025b)

Notes: DVA = Domestic value added – the portion of exports produced domestically that contributes directly to the gross domestic product; FVA = Foreign value added – inputs imported from abroad that do not add to national income; N/A = not available.

Table 7 Indonesia's coffee export destinations (2012–2022).

A. Unroasted Coffee (HS 090111)

Destination countries	Total trade value (in US$ millions)	Share (percentage)
United States	3,020	25.1
Japan	968	8.06
Germany	890	7.41
Malaysia	707	5.88
Italy	701	5.83
Egypt	581	4.83

B. Coffee (HS 0901)

Destination countries	Total trade value (in US$ millions)	Share (percentage)
United States	3,150	25.6
Japan	979	7.95
Germany	891	7.24
Malaysia	765	6.21
Italy	701	5.69
Egypt	581	4.72

Source: Authors, based on OEC (2025b)

than Vietnam's (OEC, 2025d; Tampubolon et al., 2023; USDA, 2024a). Robusta coffee accounts for 80–90% of total production, thriving at low altitudes, while Arabica is grown in highland areas such as Northern Sumatra, known for specialty coffee quality. Indonesia's coffee farms are predominantly smallholder operations, averaging 1–2 hectares, with limited access to fertilisers and modern farming techniques, which affects yield and quality. Weather patterns, particularly El Niño and La Niña, play a critical role in production. Studies (e.g., Mulyati & Indrawan, 2021; Rifin & Nauly, 2020; Vicol et al., 2018) have highlighted the challenges of including smallholders within Indonesia's coffee value chain. Nestlé Indonesia primarily sources beans from its Lampung factory, while Starbucks operates through PT Sari Coffee Indonesia, a PT Mitra Adiperkasa Tbk subsidiary, under a licensing agreement. Starbucks promotes direct farmer engagement via its Coffee and Farmer Equity Practices (Starbucks Indonesia, 2025).

Table 8 The Lao People's Democratic Republic's trade in value added (in million $).

A. Agriculture and forestry

Value added\Year	2015	2016	2017	2018	2019	2020
DVA in gross exports: World	515	676	777	686	933	1,271
DVA in gross exports: ASEAN	195	250	284	296	334	390
FVA in gross exports: World	41	41	47	48	64	104
FVA in gross exports: ASEAN	N/A	N/A	N/A	N/A	N/A	N/A
DVA in foreign final demand: World	667	771	883	805	1,037	1,302
DVA in foreign final demand: ASEAN	161	191	218	233	265	294
FVA in domestic final demand: World	147	151	140	184	329	468
FVA in domestic final demand: ASEAN	54	78	63	93	210	331

B. Manufacture of food products, beverages, and tobacco products

Value added\Year	2015	2016	2017	2018	2019	2020
DVA in gross exports: World	372	305	362	315	314	300
DVA in gross exports: ASEAN	77	72	99	98	107	91
FVA in gross exports: World	76	48	63	57	63	86
FVA in gross exports: ASEAN	N/A	N/A	N/A	N/A	N/A	N/A
DVA in foreign final demand: World	150	131	154	139	145	136
DVA in foreign final demand: ASEAN	27	26	34	35	40	35
FVA in domestic final demand: World	74	94	80	95	113	128
FVA in domestic final demand: ASEAN	24	54	36	46	56	73

Source: Authors, based on OECD (2025b)

Notes: DVA = Domestic value added – the portion of exports produced domestically that contributes directly to the gross domestic product; FVA = Foreign value added – inputs imported from abroad that do not add to national income; N/A = not available.

2.2.2 The Lao PDR

The Lao PDR has the smallest trade values among the four countries, indicating a limited role in international markets. Its trade is concentrated within ASEAN, relying on regional partners rather than global exports. Production remains locally sourced, with a low dependency on foreign inputs, reflecting a reliance on domestic agricultural resources (Table 8). While the Lao PDR's coffee exports are smaller than Indonesia's or Vietnam's, it was the fourth-largest coffee exporter in Southeast Asia in 2022, contributing 14.6% to GDP.

Table 9 The Lao People's Democratic Republic's coffee export destinations (2012–2022).

A. Unroasted Coffee (HS 090111)

Destination countries	Total trade value (in US$ millions)	Share (percentage)
Vietnam	403	39.3
Japan	166	16.2
Germany	113	11
Thailand	80	7.79
Italy	32.7	3.19
Belgium	32.5	3.17

B. Coffee (HS 0901)

Destination countries	Total trade value (in US$ millions)	Share (percentage)
Vietnam	424	39.1
Japan	166	15.3
Germany	114	10.5
Thailand	100	9.24
Italy	32.7	3.02
Belgium	32.6	3.01

Source: Authors, based on OEC (2025b)

By 2023, exports grew to $67.4 million, making it the 42nd-largest coffee exporter globally. Most coffee production takes place on the Bolaven Plateau, which spans the provinces of Champasak, Sekong, Salavan, and Attapeu (Phimmavong et al., 2023; Wongpit et al., 2023).

In 2022, the Lao PDR exported $54.77 million worth of coffee, primarily to Vietnam (Table 9), which accounted for over 50% of the Lao PDR's total exports since 2019 (OEC, 2025f). By 2023, Japan and Germany became other significant destinations (ITC, 2021). Coffee remains a crucial economic sector, contributing to GDP and rural employment. Coffee collectors act as intermediaries between producers and exporters, accessing farms through relationships with farmers and operating under trust-based agreements similar to those found in Indonesia's model. They sell red cherries or dry parchment and screen for defects. Government agencies, including the Ministry of Industry and Commerce and the Ministry of Agriculture and Forestry, support production and market access through regulations and technical assistance. Recent improvements in the coffee value chain stem from public and private training programmes (Wongpit et al., 2023).

2.2.3 Thailand

Thailand ranks high in food manufacturing, benefiting from its well-developed processing sector. It has deep global market integration, with strong foreign final demand, particularly in processed foods. The country imports significant raw materials for value-added exports, reflecting high FVA dependency (Table 10). Despite not being a major player in the global coffee supply chain, Thailand's local coffee industry stands out for its specialty and single-origin beans, particularly from Chiang Mai, Chiang Rai, and Mae Hong Son. Community-driven initiatives have improved processing practices, with individuals like Ake Suwanno revolutionising methods in Chiang Mai (Azavedo, 2024; Doi Chaang Coffee, 2025; Maspul, 2024; Newbery Street Coffee Roasters, 2025).

In 2021, Thailand's coffee industry contributed 8.8% to the country's GDP, with exports totalling $4.66 billion, primarily to Cambodia, Canada, the Netherlands, and the US (Table 11). Between 2020 and 2021, Chinese, Dutch, and Japanese markets saw the fastest growth in Thai coffee imports. In 2022, domestic coffee demand reached 91,036 tons, while production was only 18,054 tons, resulting in a supply deficit. By 2023, total production had risen slightly to 18,689 tons, with nearly equal output of Arabica (9,135 tons) and Robusta (9,554 tons). Robusta cultivation declined, while Arabica production grew by 3.2% annually, driven by global demand for premium coffee. Two Thai brands, Doi Tung and Doi Chaang, received geographical trademarks from the European Commission, recognising their unique flavours and origins (Embassy of Brazil in Bangkok, 2021). Thailand's coffee processing sector is dominated by large multinational and local companies, including Quality Coffee Products Ltd., the original equipment manufacturer (OEM) for Nestlé from 1990 to 2024 (Bangkok Post, 2025; Nestlé Thailand, 2025). As of 2022, Thailand imported 61,982 tons of unroasted coffee beans, primarily from Vietnam (70% of imports), the Lao PDR, and Indonesia. Imports totalled 5,424 million baht, underscoring the country's reliance on external sources (OEC, 2025c).

2.2.4 Vietnam

Vietnam has a strong trade in value-added products, particularly in agriculture and food processing, making it highly integrated into global supply chains. It has high foreign final demand, indicating a strong dependence on domestic

Table 10 Thailand's trade in value added (in million $).

A. Agriculture and forestry

Value added\year	2015	2016	2017	2018	2019	2020
DVA in gross exports: World	3,154	3,262	3,621	3,918	3,911	3,781
DVA in gross exports: ASEAN	387	499	598	665	691	740
FVA in gross exports: World	595	535	582	648	571	526
FVA in gross exports: ASEAN	N/A	N/A	N/A	N/A	N/A	N/A
DVA in foreign final demand: World	11,446	11,869	13,364	14,219	14,377	12,118
DVA in foreign final demand: ASEAN	1,409	1,641	1,800	2,159	2,082	1,708
FVA in domestic final demand: World	4,801	4,487	4,888	5,629	5,613	4,968
FVA in domestic final demand: ASEAN	1,071	1,151	1,296	1,459	1,419	1,279

B. Manufacture of food products, beverages, and tobacco products

Value added\year	2015	2016	2017	2018	2019	2020
DVA in gross exports: World	18,417	18,875	20,717	22,419	22,318	20,355
DVA in gross exports: ASEAN	2,835	3,353	3,533	4,555	4,085	3,336
FVA in gross exports: World	5,271	4,900	5,305	5,944	5,286	4,592
FVA in gross exports: ASEAN	N/A	N/A	N/A	N/A	N/A	N/A
DVA in foreign final demand: World	8,369	8,717	9,737	10,513	10,603	8,827
DVA in foreign final demand: ASEAN	1,134	1,343	1,435	1,831	1,688	1,278
FVA in domestic final demand: World	2,568	2,328	2,568	3,024	3,015	2,544
FVA in domestic final demand: ASEAN	464	483	535	604	574	528

Source: Authors, based on OECD (2025b)

Notes: DVA = Domestic value added – the portion of exports produced domestically that contributes directly to the gross domestic product; FVA = Foreign value added – inputs imported from abroad that do not add to national income; N/A = not available.

Table 11 Thailand's coffee export destinations (2012–2022).

A. Unroasted coffee (HS 090111)

Destination countries	Total trade value (in US$ millions)	Share (percentage)
Canada	6.96	14.8
United States	6.87	14.6
Germany	5.73	12.2
Sweden	5.37	11.4
Japan	4.23	8.98
Vietnam	3.86	8.19

B. Coffee (HS 0901)

Destination countries	Total trade value (in US$ millions)	Share (percentage)
United States	7.97	10.6
Canada	7.3	9.69
Japan	6.24	8.29
Germany	5.93	7.88
Sweden	5.86	7.77
Cambodia	5.16	6.84

Source: Authors, based on OEC (2025b)

consumption for exports. Its ASEAN trade remains active, though global markets dominate (Table 12). Vietnam is the largest coffee exporter in Southeast Asia, with coffee accounting for 11.9% of its GDP in 2022. Over 90% of exports consist of Robusta coffee. In 2021, exports were valued at $ 2.34 billion, primarily destined for Germany, the US, Italy, Japan, and Spain (Table 13). Vietnam has 113 coffee processing and exporting companies, but only one-third can export green coffee. The country has 100 processing facilities that handle 1.5 million tons of green coffee annually, and 600 establishments produce powdered coffee with a capacity of 73,000 tons. Small-scale operations account for 50% of these facilities (ICO, 2025; OEC, 2025e; TradeInt, 2024; USDA, 2024b).

Companies like Vinacafe and Trung Nguyen have invested in deep processing, but the technology remains limited due to high investment costs and financial constraints. Most factories focus on preliminary processing, limiting Vietnam's role in the global coffee value chain. Existing

Table 12 Vietnam's trade in value added (in million $).

A. Agriculture and forestry

Value added\year	2015	2016	2017	2018	2019	2020
DVA in gross exports: World	6,020	6,552	7,212	7,471	7,763	8,303
DVA in gross exports: ASEAN	513	477	460	639	557	590
FVA in gross exports: World	2,626	3,064	3,726	3,919	4,083	4,327
FVA in gross exports: ASEAN	N/A	N/A	N/A	N/A	N/A	N/A
DVA in foreign final demand: World	10,948	11,878	13,042	13,924	14,579	15,022
DVA in foreign final demand: ASEAN	915	891	875	1,213	1,273	1,223
FVA in domestic final demand: World	5,190	5,482	6,149	6,451	7,349	7,471
FVA in domestic final demand: ASEAN	963	1,077	1,209	1,366	1,522	1,585

B. Manufacture of food products, beverages, and tobacco products

Value added\Year	2015	2016	2017	2018	2019	2020
DVA in gross exports: World	6,319	6,531	8,317	8,714	9,099	9,609
DVA in gross exports: ASEAN	1,438	1,276	1,316	1,766	1,991	1,917
FVA in gross exports: World	4,041	4,190	4,726	5,001	5,232	5,383
FVA in gross exports: ASEAN	N/A	N/A	N/A	N/A	N/A	N/A
DVA in foreign final demand: World	2,064	2,159	2,348	2,683	3,052	3,073
DVA in foreign final demand: ASEAN	437	404	411	568	643	610
FVA in domestic final demand: World	6,020	6,552	7,212	7,471	7,763	8,303
FVA in domestic final demand: ASEAN	359.3	459.4	496.8	532.7	596.8	701.9

Source: Authors, based on OECD (2025b)

Notes: DVA = Domestic value added – the portion of exports produced domestically that contributes directly to the gross domestic product; FVA = Foreign value added – inputs imported from abroad that do not add to national income; N/A = not available.

Table 13 Vietnam's coffee export destinations (2012–2022).

A. Unroasted Coffee (HS 090111)

Destination countries	Total trade value (in US$ millions)	Share (percentage)
Germany	4,760	15.7
United States	3,720	12.2
Italy	2,710	8.91
Spain	2,240	7.37
Japan	1,880	6.19
Belgium	1,490	4.91

B. Coffee (HS 0901)

Destination countries	Total trade value (in US$ millions)	Share (percentage)
Germany	4,800	15.2
United States	4,070	12.9
Italy	2,710	8.62
Spain	2,450	7.78
Japan	1,920	6.09
Belgium	1,510	4.81

Source: Authors, based on OEC (2025b)

research highlights that Vietnam's failure to expand into downstream GVCs is primarily due to high investment costs (i.e., financial constraints) and the lack of coordinated support within its national innovation system for the coffee industry to enter the premium market. Vietnam is primarily known for its volume, mostly Robusta beans, rather than the quality of its coffee exports (Thăng, 2022; Vietnam Investment Review, 2025). Vietnamese coffee is valued more for its volume than for its quality, which keeps bean prices low. Green coffee exports account for the majority, while deep-processed products make up 12%. Processed coffee exports totalled $1.18 billion in 2024, marking a shift toward value-added products. However, export container shortages are likely to increase freight costs, further impacting trade. Vietnam faces intense competition from Brazil (Thăng, 2022). While Vietnam mainly sources coffee domestically, it imports raw beans from Cambodia, Indonesia, and the Lao PDR (OEC, 2025e).

2.3 Case Study: Challenges in Upgrading Smallholder Farmers in Indonesia

Integrating smallholder farmers into GVCs presents opportunities and challenges, particularly in agriculture. While GVC participation offers benefits such as market access, higher income, and comparative advantage, farmers must navigate complex quality standards, technological advancements, and power imbalances. In Indonesia, these global challenges are intensified by structural inequities and local governance dynamics, which hinder value chain upgrading. In addition, Indonesia continues to frame agribusiness policy around self-sufficiency, linking coffee to national security and resilience while emphasising local processing (OECD, 2023a, 2025a). Yet farmers remain excluded from downstream value creation, locked into volatile Robusta markets dominated by multinational roasters. While farmers in Vietnam also remain tied to Robusta exports, its state-led industrial upgrading has expanded processing capacity. Therefore, Indonesia's reliance on self-sufficiency rhetoric without redistribution is the more revealing case of structural asymmetry. This section examines the barriers to upgrading for smallholder coffee farmers, drawing insights from academic studies and fieldwork data to illuminate systemic obstacles and broader implications for rural development.

2.3.1 Understanding the Network Complexities

Global agricultural markets are shaped by power dynamics and complexities, with the coffee trade exemplifying these challenges. Non-coffee-producing countries, such as Germany and Belgium, serve as key intermediaries, potentially disadvantaging coffee-producing countries, including major producers in Latin America and Southeast Asia (Suryana et al., 2023; Utrilla-Catalan et al., 2022; Zana & Abayneh, 2019). Upgrading within GVCs requires farmers to meet evolving market demands, enhance product quality, adopt new technologies, and comply with stringent regulations. Public–private alliances also play a crucial role in addressing barriers to industry development (Fernandez-Stark et al., 2012).

Despite efforts to upgrade, rural development benefits have yet to materialise in Indonesia (Vicol et al., 2018). Roaster interventions at production sites often fail to align with rural actors' livelihood decisions, benefiting local elites (i.e., local producers who are already well positioned socially and economically) rather than smallholder farmers, who often remain marginalised from upgrading opportunities. At worst, these interventions reinforce patterns of exclusion and inequality (Vicol et al., 2018). Interviews with local actors (see Section 2.3.2) also highlight similar issues, where smallholder farmers often have limited access to prominent national-level actors (e.g., government and banks) and international-level actors (e.g., foreign buyers). Developing country governments are urged to support local upgrading through infrastructure, technology, and administrative assistance. Small and medium-sized producers face competitiveness bottlenecks, including low productivity, poor product quality, compliance barriers, and high transaction costs (Fernandez-Stark et al., 2012).

Power in the global coffee value chain has shifted to downstream firms, such as roasters and retailers, leaving farmers vulnerable to low prices while consumers pay high ones (Utrilla-Catalan et al., 2022). Market concentration has increased, with Brazil, Colombia, and Vietnam dominating exports. Non-coffee -producing nations, such as Belgium and Germany, have become essential intermediaries (Utrilla-Catalan et al., 2022). Grabs and Ponter (2019) criticise GVC studies for overlooking power inequalities between Northern buyers and Southern producers, arguing that upgrading does not always result in better value capture or regional development.

Indonesia's coffee value chain follows a standard pathway from farmers to exporters and processors; however, regional disparities affect the distribution of value. Studies highlight issues from technology adoption and standard practices to trade-related challenges, including market access limitations due to intermediary dependency (Mulyati & Indrawan, 2021; Suryana et al., 2023; Vicol et al., 2018). Due to poor coordination, smallholder farmers struggle with power asymmetries, uneven benefit distribution, and inefficient government policies (Figure 4).

2.3.2 A Deep Dive into the Local Actors in Indonesia

As presented in Section 2.2, Indonesia is the second-largest coffee exporter in Southeast Asia. However, their export of raw coffee beans is far below Vietnam's, while their specialty coffee development is less well known than Thailand's. In Indonesia, most coffee plantations are located on Sumatra Island. The coffee beans from that area are also famous. The inability of smallholder farmers in Indonesia to expand and upgrade within the global coffee value chain is due to the presence of the 'hidden middle' or intermediaries. Interviews conducted with smallholder farmers and small-scale collectors in Dairi, North Sumatra, in 2022, and another interview with a small-scale exporter in Surabaya, East Java, in 2024, confirmed the findings from existing studies (Kresnawati, 2024; Sinaga, 2022; Sudiono, 2022; Tumangger & Mulyadi, 2022).

Interviews conducted in 2022 and 2024 reveal critical insights into interactions among local actors in Indonesia's coffee sector. At the regional level,

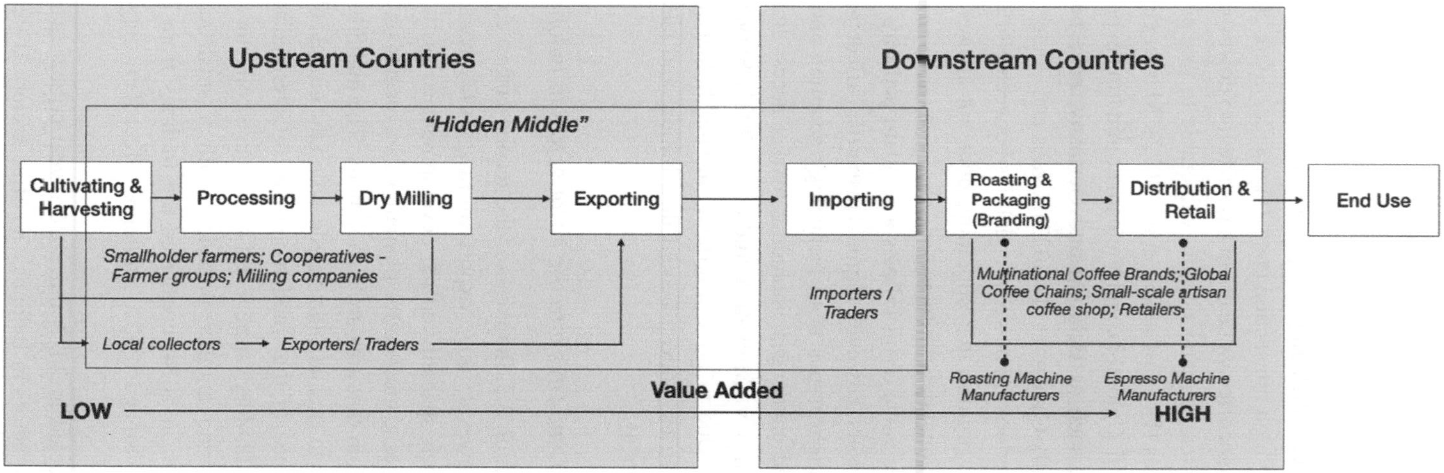

Figure 4 Global coffee value chain.

Source: Authors, based on Fernandez-Stark et al. (2012), Gereffi et al. (2005), ITC (2021), and the interviews in Section 2.3.2.

rural governments and Village-Owned Enterprises (BUMDes), which are managed by the community, provide machinery and financial assistance, such as grants, to support farmer groups and small-scale farmers. However, this decentralised approach often leads to inefficiencies in policy implementation, as the chain of command between the Departments of Agriculture and Trade lacks cohesion. While Sumatra is renowned for coffee plantations (e.g., Aceh, Mandailing, and Dairi coffee), Java's coffee plantations, such as those in Dampit, are smaller in scale and dispersed. Regardless of location, smallholder farmers typically sell their green coffee beans to trusted large-scale coffee collectors and exporters, who are predominantly traders rather than producer–exporters. These transactions often occur without formal contracts, limiting farmers' ability to secure stable market conditions (Kresnawati, 2024).

At the provincial level, government support is primarily directed toward traders by facilitating connections between buyers through business matching programmes. However, most recipients of these programmes are traders rather than producer–exporters due to the limited number of the latter and the small-scale nature of coffee production. Exporters face challenges meeting the high demand for coffee beans in export markets and must source from multiple plantations due to inadequate supply. Compounding this issue is the preference of many Indonesian coffee companies and cafés for imported coffee beans, which are often cheaper, resulting in the booming café culture providing little direct benefit to small-scale farmers. Small-scale farmers, in turn, prioritise immediate economic needs over exporting or upgrading their operations (Sinaga, 2022; Sudiono, 2022; Tumangger & Mulyadi, 2022).

Intermediaries, such as coffee collectors and traders, play a pivotal role by controlling access to critical market information and technological support. While these intermediaries maintain transactional relationships with smallholder farmers, they rarely provide training or share knowledge to help farmers meet export standards. Provincial governments also selectively provide information to traders, often based on personal connections, further excluding farmers from growth opportunities. Local governments occasionally host workshops or provide machinery to farmers (Kresnawati, 2024; Sinaga, 2022).

An effective national innovation system requires a multistakeholder and multisectoral approach, especially to address issues in the global coffee value chain, such as sustainability issues and other global standardisations (OECD, 2025a). Experiences from East Asian developmental states, such as Japan, South Korea, and Taiwan, highlight the critical role of universities in developing technologies that support farmers' integration into GVCs. In the coffee sector, partnerships with universities provide access to innovations that strengthen production capacities, such as climate adaptation, pest management, and post-harvest techniques (Gabriel & Lubis, 2025; Lalu et al., 2025; OECD, 2023a; Onyas et al., 2018). Universities also build farmers' knowledge and organisational capacity, though their impact is limited in addressing short-term challenges like bypassing intermediaries or securing higher prices. Farmers still require business partnerships to gain market access and investment, since universities rarely purchase coffee directly (ICO, 2024; Sachs et al., 2019). In addition, there are existing issues related to universities' limited capacity to connect farmers with businesses in Southeast Asia, which hinder the effectiveness of knowledge-transfer mechanisms (Ha et al., 2025; Kresnawati, 2024). At the regional level, an unfinished academic network initiative in Southeast Asia seeks to advance a multi-actor and multi-stakeholder approach to addressing the unsustainable agri-food system (Nelles, 2023). Nevertheless, for the triple helix model to succeed, university interventions must extend beyond sustainability concerns to confront financial and logistical intermediary constraints that currently undermine effective coordination (BASIC, 2018, 2024).

2.4 Conclusion

GVC participation helps high-value agricultural sectors, such as coffee, boost productivity and economic growth. Farmers must upgrade from low-value tasks, such as farming, to higher-value processes, such as roasting, branding, and refinement. While specialty coffee offers higher income, it also poses challenges for small producers. Currently, exporters transport most of the coffee trade as green beans. It is essential to note that roasting requires specialised machinery, and roasted coffee beans have a shorter lifespan. Roasting is a value-added activity typically done closer to consumer markets. Agricultural value chains are buyer-driven, with brands and traders controlling design, marketing, and sales while outsourcing production. Green coffee beans are mostly exported from developing countries, where roasting and processing add value. European manufacturers dominate the production of coffee machinery, including roasting and espresso machines.

Vietnam leads Southeast Asia's coffee exports, relying mainly on Robusta coffee but struggling with limited processing infrastructure. Indonesia, the region's second-largest exporter, faces uncoordinated government efforts to boost exports. Despite smaller export volumes, the Lao PDR depends on coffee exports to Thailand and Vietnam. Thailand has gained recognition in specialty coffee, particularly single-origin beans from Chiang Mai, Chiang Rai, and Mae Hong Son.

Across the region, intermediaries – that is, coffee collectors and traders – control market access and information, often operating based on trust-based agreements. While Southeast Asia has success stories in specialty coffee, limited processing facilities and reliance on intermediaries hinder industry growth. Interviews with farmers and exporters in Sumatra and Java highlight how the 'hidden middle' rarely shares knowledge or technology with producers. Local governments provide equipment and workshops, but efforts remain fragmented and poorly coordinated. Provincial governments support traders over producer–exporters, restricting market access for farmers. The booming café culture and preference for cheaper imported beans further limit the benefits of small-scale farmers.

Designing a policy recommendation to enhance Southeast Asian participation to a higher level of value added within the global coffee value chain is a complex task. Existing studies have identified key policy priorities, ranging from providing financial support (i.e., strategic investment) to facilitating smallholder farmers' direct access to international markets (i.e., foreign buyers). Yet, we have to recognise the systemic complexities that exist both from the buyer's side (i.e., the market in the developed countries) and from the producers' side (i.e., producers in developing countries), such as the number of actors involved and their relationships (e.g., the way they conduct the transactions, the trust system, and who gains access to government's supports). These complexities contribute to the limited effectiveness of various intervention schemes. Nevertheless, to begin with, it is essential to address the existing power asymmetry by including smallholder farmers at decision-making levels and in contract discussions, as well as by improving the regulation of intermediaries (i.e., the hidden middle). Second, this needs to be followed by a strategic investment in processing infrastructure and technology. Third, at the regional level, standards harmonisation may be beneficial to ASEAN (e.g., quality protocols and training benchmarks across member states and promoting regional coffee origins). However, a universal policy approach remains challenging, as Southeast Asian countries differ significantly in local customs, institutional contexts, and, most importantly, their geographical conditions.

3 Textile and Clothing

3.1 Introduction

The rise of ASEAN in T&C GVCs is remarkable. Over the last three decades, ASEAN has positioned itself as a key segment of the global production network. While figures vary depending on the data and methodology used, historical trends consistently indicate that the T&C sector has maintained a relatively high level of GVC involvement among labour-intensive sectors in ASEAN (ASEAN-Japan Centre, 2019). The analysis indicates that, on average, the region's backward participation is around 33%, while forward participation is much more limited, at around 7% at the end of the period 1995 – 2020.[3] Evidence shows that participation in GVC has significantly enhanced export growth, created job opportunities, and improved income and productivity levels in this area (Winkler, 2022; Yunas et al., 2024).

Although GVC participation remained high, ASEAN's T&C sector was already at a crossroads. While the region remains highly integrated into GVCs, the share of value added in assembly and basic manufacturing tasks is declining, with higher-value activities increasingly concentrated in advanced economies (Chang et al., 2016; Winkler, 2022; Yamaguchi, 2018). Moreover, opportunities for upgrading and linkage development remain relatively restrained in ASEAN, given the nature of the value chain and their limited engagement in textile or fibre production (Chang et al., 2016). These dynamics underscore the urgency for ASEAN to transition from assembly-based roles to innovation-driven, higher-value activities to sustain competitiveness.

This section focuses on the ASEAN T&C industry, the key challenges in maintaining its position within the GVC, and the policy implications for sectoral sustainability. The purpose of this section is twofold. The primary objective is to analyse the participation of ASEAN countries in the GVCs of the T&C sector, examining both backward and forward linkages to understand their impact on productivity improvements and sustainable upgrading outcomes (Hue & Korwatanasakul, 2023; Tian et al., 2022). The second aim of this section is to identify systematic challenges faced by these countries in sustaining their GVC positions during global competition and regional geopolitical intensification, declining value addition, and pressures to meet social and environmental standards (Barrientos et al., 2011) to guide future GVC-related policymaking and secure a more sustainable role in the global T&C production network of ASEAN countries.

3.2 Mapping the Development of T&C GVC in ASEAN

3.2.1 T&C Trade in ASEAN: A Brief Overview

ASEAN's textile trade has undergone significant evolution over the past decade. Tables 14 and 15 summarise ASEAN's trade composition of textiles (HS52, 54, 55, 58, 59, and 60) and clothing products (HS61, 62, and 63). On the export side, finished garments (HS 61–62) have remained the core strength of the region, consistently contributing the majority of export value, around 80% in 2012–2015 and still dominant in 2021–2024, despite a modest decline in share. This

[3] Simple average of backward and forward participation values across ten ASEAN countries.

Table 14 Export composition of textile and clothing products in major ASEAN countries.

HS code	Description	2012–2015 Average (%)	2021–2024 Average (%)	Change (p.p.)
61	Knitted Apparel	42.20%	30.60%	↓ −11.6
62	Woven Apparel	35.20%	27.70%	↓ −7.5
63	Other Textile Articles	4.50%	5.20%	↑ +0.7
56	Wadding/Nonwovens	2.10%	5.30%	↑ +3.2
60	Knitted Fabrics	1.90%	4.50%	↑ +2.6
57–59	Other Intermediate Goods	14.10%	26.70%	↑ +12.6

Source: Authors, based on UNCOMTRADE

Table 15 Import composition of textile and clothing products in major ASEAN countries.

HS code	Description	2012–2015 Average (%)	2021–2024 Average (%)	Change (p.p.)
52	Cotton	39.3%	14.7%	↓ −24.6
54	Man-made Filaments	24.5%	19.5%	↓ −5.0
55	Man-made Staple Fibres	29.8%	15.5%	↓ −14.3
60	Knitted Fabrics	1.2%	7.3%	↑ +6.1
61–63	Finished Garments/ Textiles	2.7%	39.0%	↑ +36.3

Source: Authors, based on UNCOMTRADE

reflects ASEAN's comparative advantage in labour-intensive manufacturing and its continued integration into global apparel supply chains.

However, the import structure shifted in a less unfavourable direction. The share of finished garment imports rose sharply between 2012 and 2015 and again between 2021 and 2024, while imports of upstream materials declined. This trend may reflect growing competition from China, driven by geopolitical disruptions and shifts in sourcing strategies by global brands. The influx of low-cost finished goods has put pressure on domestic producers, contributing to factory closures and job losses in some ASEAN countries.[4]

[4] The relaxation of import restrictions on ready-made garments in Indonesia, for example, has been linked to factory closures and approximately 13,800 layoffs in 2024 as local firms struggle to

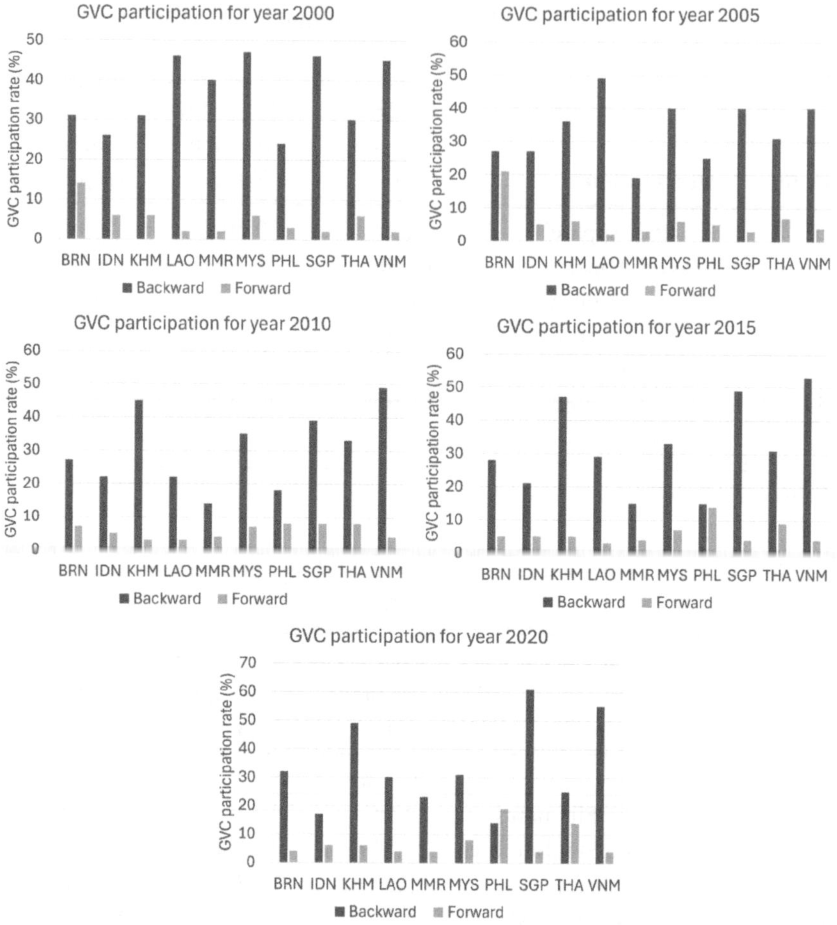

Figure 5 GVC participation- backward and forward linkages.

Source: Authors, based on OECD's TIVA database, version 2023

Note: BRN = Brunei Darussalam; IDN = Indonesia; KHM = Cambodia; LAO = Lao PDR; MMR = Myanmar; MYS = Malaysia; PHL = Philippines; SGP = Singapore; THA = Thailand; VNM = Vietnam. OECD's industrial classification includes textiles, garments, and footwear.

3.2.2 Dynamics of GVC Participation in ASEAN's T&C Industry

Figure 5 shows the evolution of backward and forward GVC participation in the textile, garment, and footwear sector across ASEAN between 1995 and 2020. The period is divided into three sub-periods: 1995 to 2005, when the Multi-Fibre

compete with cheaper imports (Cahyoputra, 2024). Furthermore, analysts describe this dynamic as an emerging 'China shock' in ASEAN, with inexpensive Chinese imports contributing to factory closures and job losses in various sectors, textile being one of them (Raychaudhuri, 2025).

Arrangement expired; 2006 to 2011; and 2012 to 2020. The period averages indicate a clear reorganisation of ASEAN's textile GVC participation, characterised by rising backward participation and limited forward participation. At the ASEAN level, average backward participation increases from 32.6% in 1995–2005 to 33.1% in 2006–2011, and further to 34.6% in 2012–2020. In contrast, forward participation rises more modestly, from 4.4% to 5.8% and 6.3% across the same periods. This widening gap indicates that deeper integration has been driven mainly by increased use of imported intermediate inputs rather than by greater domestic value captured upstream or downstream.

Brunei Darussalam's textile GVC participation is volatile. Its backward participation declines from 32.2% in 1995–2005 to 24.0% in 2006–2011, before recovering to 28.1% in 2012–2020. Forward participation peaks at 18.0% in the middle period, compared with 10.7% before 2005 and 6.9% thereafter. These fluctuations suggest episodic engagement rather than a stable integration path.

Cambodia exhibits the strongest post-2005 structural shift. Backward participation rises sharply from 30.8% in 1995–2005 to 46.2% in 2006–2011 and remains high at 47.2% in 2012–2020. Forward participation, however, remains low, fluctuating between 5.5%, 3.7% and 5.8%. This divergence reflects deeper integration, concentrated in assembly activities, following the phase-out of the Multi-Fibre Arrangement.

Indonesia exhibits no clear structural break in either backward or forward participation, in contrast to the adjustments observed in other ASEAN economies. Average backward participation declines gradually from 23.3% in 1995–2005 to 22.5% in 2006–2011, and then to 20.3% in 2012–2020. Forward participation remains stable at around 5–5.5% across all periods. Given the major reorganisation of global textile supply chains after 2005, this persistence suggests limited responsiveness rather than structural stability.

The Lao PDR maintains consistently high backward participation even though it declines, averaging 41.6% in 1995–2005, 34.0% in 2006–2011, and 31.1% in 2012–2020, alongside negligible forward participation of 2.3–3.3% across periods. Despite fluctuations, the data indicate persistent dependence on imported inputs and weak domestic linkages.

Malaysia combines high backward participation with gradual gains in forward participation. Backward participation declines from 42.2% in 1995–2005 to 36.2% in 2006–2011 and 33.2% in 2012–2020, while forward participation rises from 5.6% to 6.8% and 7.6%. This indicates incremental progress toward higher-value-added functions alongside sustained regional integration.

Myanmar's backward participation declines from 28.7% in 1995–2005 to 16.8% in 2006–2011, before partially recovering to 20.6% in 2012–2020. Forward participation increases modestly from 2.3% to 3.8% and 4.4% but remains low in absolute terms. This pattern suggests delayed and shallow integration with limited upgrading.

The Philippines follows a contrasting trajectory. Backward participation declines steadily from 26.2% in 1995–2005 to 20.2% in 2006–2011 and 15.4% in 2012–2020, while forward participation increases sharply from 3.4% to 6.8% and then to 14.9%. This shift suggests a reorientation away from assembly toward downstream and service-related activities.

Singapore records persistently high backward participation, rising from 40.6% in 1995–2005 to 41.0% in 2006–2011 and 48.1% in 2012–2020. Forward participation increases modestly from 2.5% to 6.2%, before stabilising at 4.2%. Given limited domestic production, this reflects Singapore's role as a logistics and coordination hub rather than as a manufacturing hub.

Thailand shows evidence of partial functional upgrading. Backward participation increases from 26.8% in 1995–2005 to 33.0% in 2006–2011, then declines to 30.1% in 2012–2020. Forward participation rises steadily from 6.0% to 8.2% and 9.8%, indicating a gradual shift toward higher-value-added activities.

Vietnam exhibits a strong and sustained deepening of backward integration. Backward participation rose from 39.7% in 1995–2005 to 47.2% in 2006–2011 and 52.8% in 2012–2020, the highest in ASEAN. Forward participation remains flat at around 4% throughout. This pattern reflects rapid scale expansion in downstream production driven by imported inputs, with limited evidence of upstream or downstream upgrading.

Overall, the figures confirm a clear structural break around the mid 2000s, followed by consolidation after 2012. ASEAN's textile GVC integration has intensified primarily through downstream assembly, while functional upgrading remains uneven and concentrated in a small number of more advanced economies.

Number of Firms

Table 16 presents data on textile and garment establishments in ASEAN from 2015 to 2020. In 2015, Vietnam had 6,990 establishments, positioning it as a major producer alongside Malaysia (8,736) and Indonesia (4,972). The Philippines (755) and Singapore (451) had smaller numbers, while Myanmar and Brunei Darussalam recorded 21 and 333, respectively, highlighting a tiered industry structure.

By 2020, Vietnam had nearly doubled its number of establishments to 13,228, driven by increased GVC integration and foreign investment. It is worth noting that, despite the significant increase in the number of firms (Figure 5), Vietnam still specialises in low-value-added downstream stages,

Table 16 Number of firms in the textile and garment sector.

A. 2015

Country	Number of firms
Brunei Darussalam	333
Indonesia	4,972
Lao PDR	510
Malaysia	8,736
Myanmar	21
Philippines	755
Singapore	451
Thailand	129,976 (2016)
Vietnam	6,990

B. 2020

Country	Number of firms
Brunei Darussalam	274
Indonesia	4,259
Lao PDR	N/A
Malaysia	8,812
Myanmar	22
Philippines	1,505
Singapore	479
Thailand	N/A
Vietnam	13,228

Source: UNIDO's INDSTAT4 Revision 4 database. Retrieved from https://stat.unido.org/data/table?dataset=indstat&revision=4#data-browser on 2nd April 2025

Note: Lao PDR = Lao People's Democratic Republic; N/A = not available

with increasing backward and limited forward GVC participation. Malaysia stayed stable at 8,812, while Indonesia declined to 4,259, possibly due to consolidation and rising import competition. The Philippines more than doubled its count to 1,505, signalling growth in formal production. Myanmar remained flat at 22, and Singapore declined further, reflecting the country's strength as a service-based economy.

Overall, the changes in establishment numbers from 2015 to 2020 reflect differing national trends in the textile and garment sector across ASEAN. These shifts suggest varying levels of industry expansion and policy or investment dynamics across the region.

Foreign Direct Investment Inflows

Figure 6 illustrates FDI capital expenditure in ASEAN's textile sector from 2012 to 2024, showing Vietnam as the dominant destination. It experienced major investment peaks in 2014 ($2.2 billion), 2016 ($1.9 billion), and 2019 ($1.5 billion), followed by a rebound to $915 million by 2024. Vietnam's appeal stems from its low labour costs, improved infrastructure, and strong GVC integration.

Indonesia ranks second, with a notable surge in 2020 ($1.1 billion), indicating episodic investor interest. Cambodia and Myanmar experienced peaks in 2014–2015, possibly due to relocations from China, followed by steep declines, likely driven by political instability and rising costs. Other countries, such as Malaysia, the Philippines, and Thailand, saw only modest and stable inflows, while the Lao PDR and Singapore attracted minimal investment.

Figure 7 tracks the number of FDI projects, reaffirming Vietnam's leadership. It recorded peaks in 2014 (25 projects), 2016 (23), and 2019 (18), followed by a COVID-19 dip and a recovery to 13 projects in 2024. Vietnam's high investment volume and project count reflect a mature ecosystem appealing to both large firms and smaller manufacturers.

Cambodia and Indonesia had fewer recurring projects. Cambodia experienced a brief surge in 2023, with eight projects likely driven by ethical investment promotion. Myanmar's activity declined post-2020, and Thailand, Malaysia, and the Philippines consistently recorded low numbers. Minimal activity in Singapore aligns with limited roles in labour-intensive production, while the small numbers in Brunei Darussalam and the Lao PDR indicate limited investor interest due to small labour forces and market sizes.

Together, the data confirm Vietnam's dual strength in attracting both high-value and frequent textile FDI. In contrast, other ASEAN countries exhibit either smaller-scale or sporadic investment, pointing to capacity gaps or investor hesitation. These trends reinforce ASEAN's dominant position in downstream GVC activities, with forward linkages still limited.

Employment

Figure 8 shows textile employment across ASEAN. In 2015, Vietnam led with 1.48 million workers, followed by Indonesia (1.2 million) and Thailand (413,000). The Philippines and Malaysia had smaller workforces

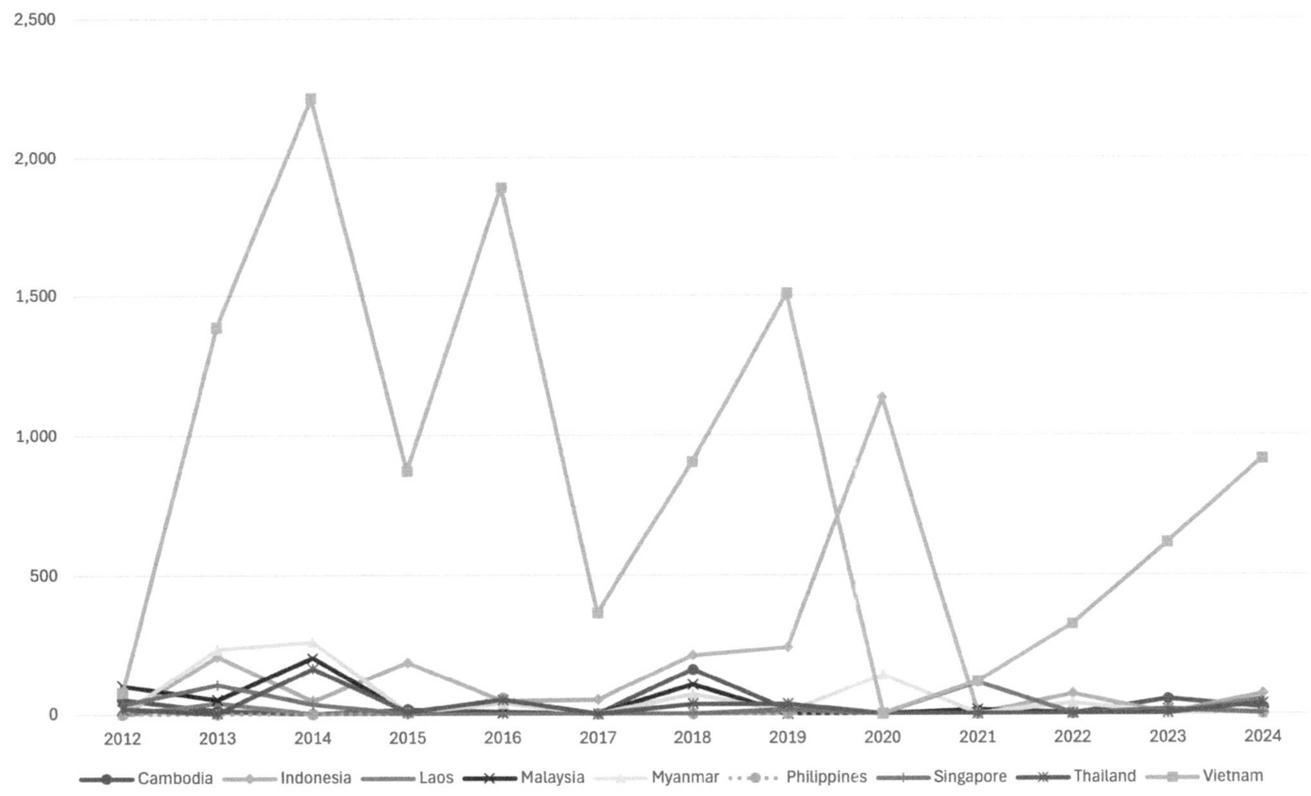

Figure 6 FDI inflows by capital investment annually.

Source: Financial Times' FDIMarkets database.
Note: Capital investment to destination countries in USD millions.

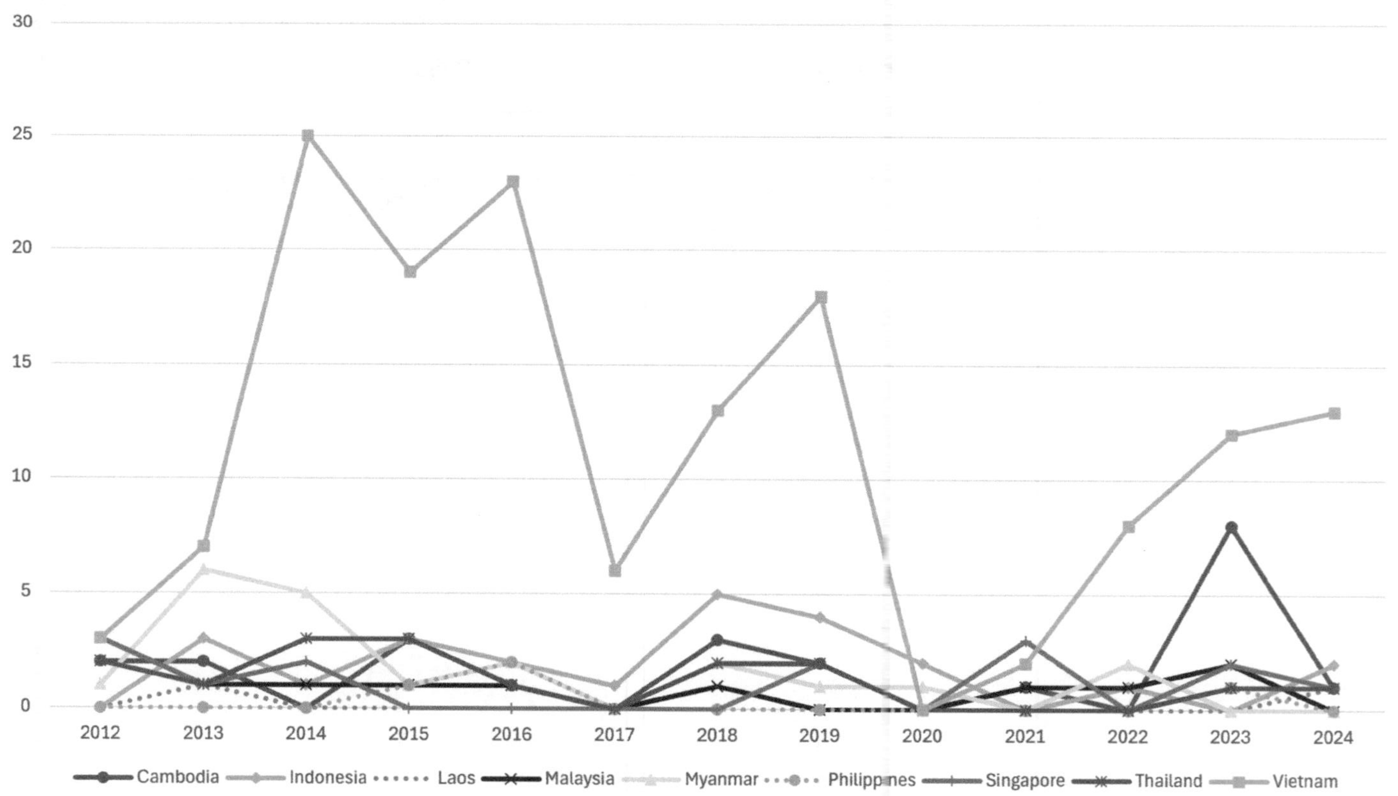

Figure 7 FDI inflows by the number of projects annually.

Source: Financial Times' FDI Markets database

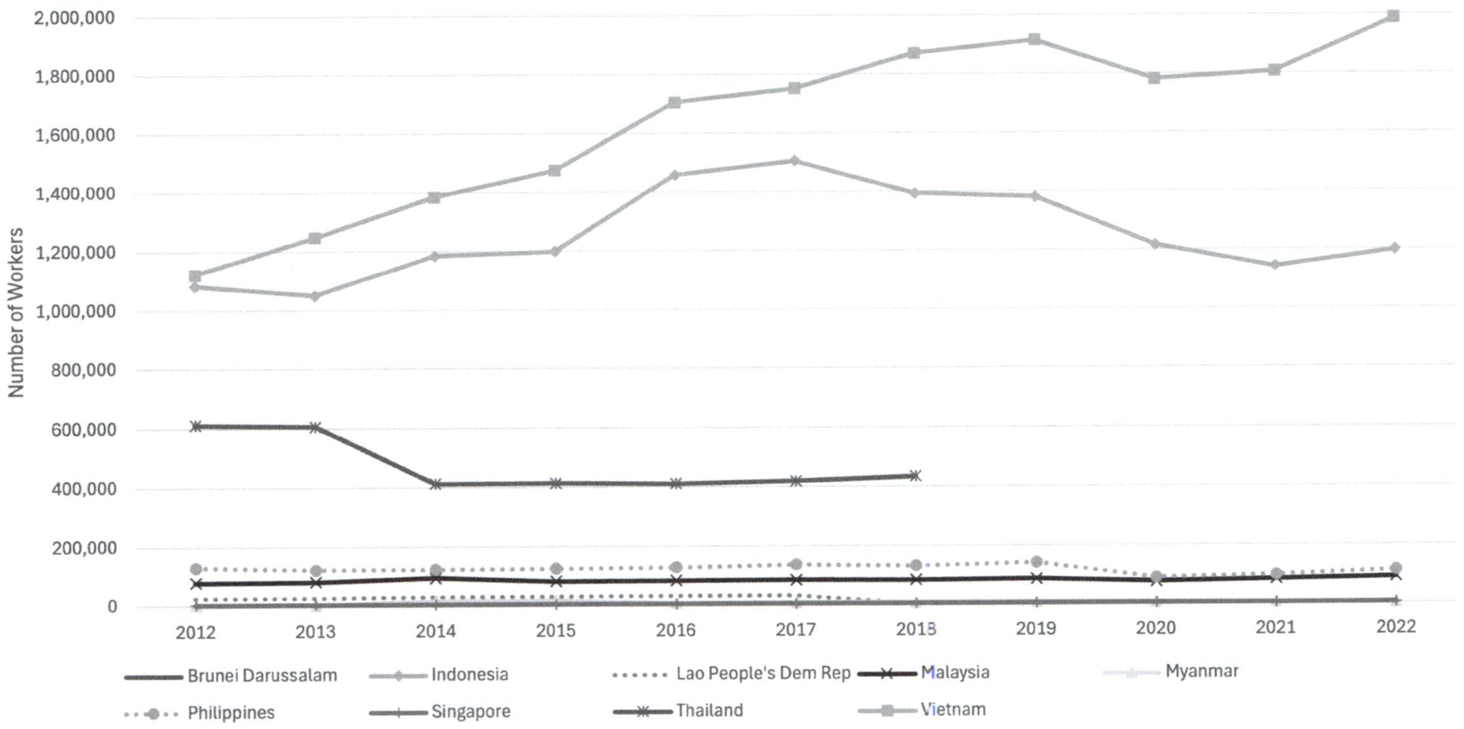

Figure 8 Employment in the textile and garment sector.

Source: UNIDO INDSTAT4 Rev.4

(125,175 and 82,411, respectively), while Brunei Darussalam and Singapore employed fewer than 3,000 workers each, reflecting the limited scale or capital-intensive nature of their production models.

By 2020, Vietnam's employment remained strong, increasing to 1.78 million despite disruptions from the pandemic. Indonesia fell slightly from its 2016 peak (1.46 million) to 1.2 million. The Philippines declined sharply to about 90,000, while Malaysia and Thailand saw only marginal changes. Myanmar's employment fell from 5,750 in 2019 to 4,674 in 2020, reflecting vulnerabilities in smaller economies.

Labour Cost Dynamics

Figure 9 presents labour cost trends from 2012 to 2022. Vietnam's average labour cost rose from $2,348 to $4,360 (compound annual growth rate (CAGR): 6.3%), driven by industrial upgrading. Indonesia also experienced significant growth, increasing from $2,195 to $3,410 (CAGR: 4.5%). Malaysia's increase was modest, rising from $5,265 to $6,559 (CAGR: 2.2%), and Thailand grew at 1.7% ($3,672 to $4,080 by 2018).

Myanmar exhibited sharp fluctuations, peaking at $3,110 in 2020 before falling to $1,651 in 2021, reflecting instability. The Philippines showed no clear upward trend. Singapore maintained the region's highest costs, but wages declined slightly (from $18,150 to $16,469; CAGR: −0.9%), indicating automation and restructuring in labour-intensive segments.

Regional Linkages

Data on intra-ASEAN linkages reveal divergent trends. Between 2012 and 2020, the average share of FVA sourced from within ASEAN declined slightly, from 11.2% to 10.7%, indicating a continued reliance on extra-regional inputs (Table 17). In contrast, DVA from within ASEAN rose from 20.4% to 28.2%, suggesting growing internal production capabilities.

The Lao PDR recorded the highest intra-ASEAN FVA shares, at 45.0% in 2012 and 43.6% in 2020, indicating strong regional sourcing. Singapore and Thailand increased their DVA shares, enhancing their contribution to regional exports. Vietnam's intra-ASEAN linkages remained below average, while Brunei Darussalam, Malaysia, and Singapore posted gains in ASEAN DVA, reflecting improved domestic integration. These trends highlight a gradual deepening of domestic production in ASEAN's textile, garment, and footwear sector, particularly in DVA, but underline the need for stronger regional sourcing of inputs to build more resilient supply chains.

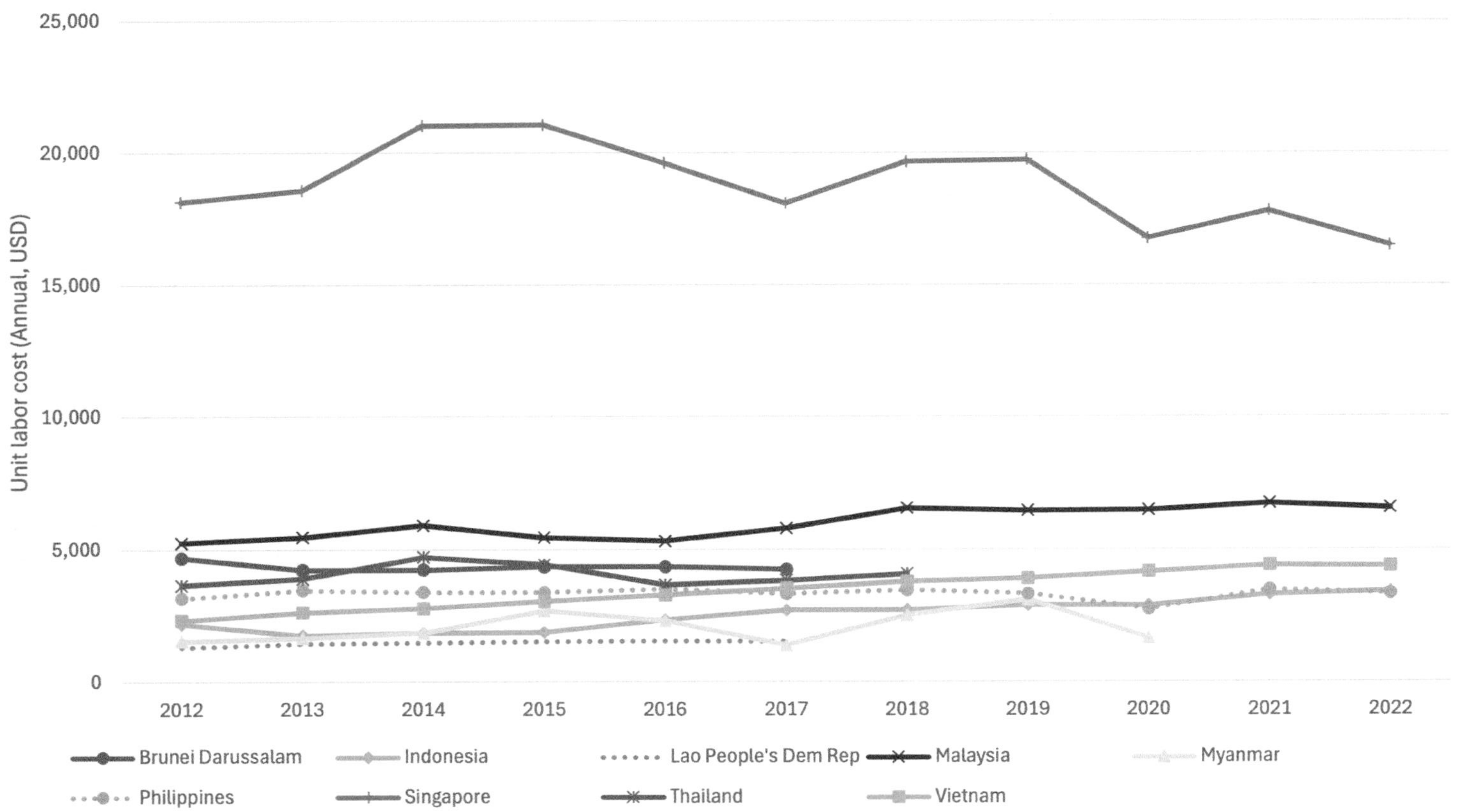

Figure 9 Unit labour cost in the textile and garment sector.

Source: UNIDO INDSTAT4 Rev.4

Table 17 Intra-ASEAN linkage.

A. 2012

Country	ASEAN FVA (% of total FVA)	ASEAN DVA (% of total DVA)
Brunei Darussalam	25.8	22.6
Indonesia	12.1	15.6
Cambodia	8.7	16.3
Lao PDR	45.1	24.5
Myanmar	17.4	24.7
Malaysia	18.0	35.8
Philippines	16.7	18.0
Singapore	14.0	28.9
Thailand	11.8	30.7
Vietnam	10.3	11.6
ASEAN Average	11.2	20.4

B. 2020

Country	ASEAN FVA (% of total FVA)	ASEAN DVA (% of total DVA)
Brunei Darussalam	21.3	38.3
Indonesia	13.4	23.2
Cambodia	15.8	19.4
Lao PDR	43.6	19.6
Myanmar	13.4	23.5
Malaysia	17.0	45.4
Philippines	15.6	23.0
Singapore	15.6	44.7
Thailand	14.0	52.2
Vietnam	9.4	16.5
ASEAN Average	10.7	28.2

Source: Authors' calculation from OECD's TiVA database.

3.2.3 T&C Industries in Three ASEAN Countries: Cambodia, Myanmar, and Vietnam

In the previous section, we have mapped the development of ASEAN's T&C sector, highlighting the region's deepening integration into GVCs, shifting trade patterns, and the varied trajectories of member states in terms of investment, employment, and regional linkages. Within this broader context, Cambodia, Myanmar, and Vietnam emerge as particularly compelling case studies due to their rapid export growth, distinct policy environments, and pivotal roles as hubs for labour-intensive garment production. These countries exemplify both the opportunities and challenges faced by ASEAN economies as they seek to move beyond low-value assembly toward greater value addition and long-term sectoral competitiveness and resilience. In this subsection, we focus on tracing the evolution of the T&C industries in Cambodia, Myanmar, and Vietnam, examining their integration into GVCs, the structure of their industries, and the implications for regional industrial transformation.

Cambodia: Low-Value Assembly Trap

Cambodia's T&C industry emerged as a critical driver of economic growth following political stabilisation in the early 1990s. Between 1995 and 2020, Cambodia's T&C exports surged from $25 million to $7.76 billion, primarily driven by the EU's Everything But Arms initiative (2001) and the US Generalised System of Preferences, which granted duty-free access to Western markets (Sovirak and Kim, 2006; World Bank, 2026a). By 2025, export earnings from textile and clothing products had reach $11.8 billion, accounting for 37.8% of Cambodia's total merchandise export, underscoring their fundamental role in the country's economic development (General Department of Customs and Excise of Cambodia, 2026),[5] underscoring their fundamental role in the country's economic development. Currently, the industry employs over 750,000 people, making it the largest formal employer in Cambodia. It primarily provides jobs for young women from rural areas, serving as a critical source of household income and remittances that underpin local economies (ASEAN Main Portal, 2024).

Cambodia's T&C sector is primarily export-oriented and highly integrated into the T&C GVCs. It is dominated by foreign-owned manufacturers, primarily from China, Hong Kong, Singapore, Malaysia, Japan and South Korea, among which China-owned firms account for approximately 90% (Natsuda et al., 2010; Ravindran, 2024). These firms mainly serve global buyers such as H&M, Adidas, and Zara, which coordinate production under buyer-driven GVC models (Gereffi, 1999; Rastogi, 2018). Local Cambodian firms, predominantly SMEs, play a marginal role, focusing on subcontracting low-value tasks such as cutting and sewing (Natsuda et al., 2010). The lack of backward linkages to domestic textile production has constrained functional upgrading, leaving Cambodia reliant on assembly roles (Bernhardt, 2013).

[5] Textile and clothing products refer to the HS categories used in the analysis: HS 61, 62, 63, 56, 60 and 57-59.

Moreover, Cambodia's T&C sector is characterised by extreme import dependency, with more than 60% of fabrics imported primarily from China (ASEAN Main Portal, 2024). Cambodia's reliance on imported inputs reflects weak backward linkages and limited investment in spinning and weaving infrastructure, perpetuating low domestic value addition (ASEAN Main Portal, 2024). Such dependency increases vulnerability to global supply chain disruptions, as seen during the COVID-19 pandemic and later reflected in the 14% drop in Cambodian textile and footware exports in 2023 (Pisei, 2024).

Cambodia's T&C sector primarily relies on low-skilled, labour-intensive activities. By 2024, the sector employed around one million workers, of whom over 75% were women (Alissar, 2025). Only a small portion of the workforce consists of highly skilled workers and professionals, primarily in managerial or supervisory roles, which positions Cambodia in the lower ranks of the global garment industry.

Myanmar: Low Value in Assembly Roles

From 1995 to 2020, Myanmar's T&C sector underwent a significant transformation shaped by economic liberalisation, integration into GVCs, and shifting geopolitical dynamics. Partial economic reforms in the early 1990s, including the opening of the sector to foreign investment and the establishment of joint ventures with Korean and Hong Kong firms, laid the groundwork for export-oriented growth. The sector expanded rapidly in the late 1990s, with the number of factories peaking at over 300 and employment reaching 300,000 by 2001, before a sharp contraction following the imposition of US sanctions in 2003 (Kudo, 2012). Recovery began in the 2010s, following the lifting of Western sanctions and the reinstatement of EU trade preferences under the Everything But Arms scheme. This significantly bolstered Myanmar's garment sector through increased FDI and export growth. The scheme offers duty-free, quota-free access to the EU market, which accounts for over half of Myanmar's garment exports. By 2023, Myanmar's T&C exports were valued at approximately \$4.46 billion, accounting for about 30.2% of the country's total exports and making it the largest export sector (World Bank, 2026b).

The sector's integration into GVCs has been characterised by limited backward linkages and reliance on imported materials, with low-value cut-make-pack activities dominating production (Eurocham Myanmar, 2023; ILO Liaison Office in Myanmar, 2015). The industry operates predominantly under the cut-make-pack model, where foreign buyers supply raw materials (e.g., fabrics, buttons, and zippers). Myanmar manufacturers are paid only for labour-intensive assembly tasks (ILO Liaison Office in Myanmar, 2015; World

Bank, 2023). This structure results in minimal domestic value addition, estimated at 30% of export value for cut-make-pack activities, compared to 70% retained by foreign buyers for inputs and branding (World Bank, 2023). Over 88% of firms source inputs from abroad, primarily via sea shipments, with only 2% reporting local fabric availability (World Bank, 2023). Such import dependency reflects weak backward linkages, as Myanmar lacks the necessary infrastructure, technical capacity, and investment to produce high-quality textiles domestically.

However, recent political instability, particularly following the 2021 military coup, has had a profound negative impact on the country's T&C sector. Estimates indicate that approximately one-third of garment factories ceased operations, resulting in the loss of over 220,000 jobs, the majority of which were held by women (ILO, 2022). A combination of international order cancellations, the withdrawal of major brands, and domestic instability collectively drove these disruptions, undermining the sector's competitiveness and ability to participate in higher-value segments of GVCs. Consequently, Myanmar's garment industry has become increasingly marginalised within global production networks, with limited prospects for recovery absent political stabilisation and the restoration of international market confidence.

Vietnam: Dual Edges of GVC Participation

Vietnam's T&C industry underwent a transformative evolution following the Doi Moi economic reforms initiated in 1986, which shifted the nation from a centralised to a market-oriented economy. The Doi Moi reforms are widely recognised as the foundation for Vietnam's transformation into one of Southeast Asia's most dynamic economies, combining market mechanisms with socialist orientation under the continued leadership of the Communist Party. Key policies included the decentralisation of economic management, the liberalisation of trade and investment, the encouragement of private enterprises, and the gradual privatisation of state-owned enterprises. The reforms also introduced an 'open door' policy, facilitating FDI and integration into global markets, while maintaining the state's strategic role in key sectors (Korwatanasakul, 2023b; Tsuboi, 2007).

These reforms, coupled with strategic integration into GVCs, have positioned Vietnam as a leading T&C exporter in Southeast Asia. From 1986 to 2024, the sector experienced exponential export growth, rising from negligible contributions to Vietnam's second-largest export category by 2023, with exports totalling \$40.3 billion in 2023, accounting for 11.4% of Vietnam's manufactured exports, and becoming a major supplier to the US, the world's largest garment market (World Bank, 2026c). The sector's rapid expansion and increasing global market share have propelled Vietnam to become the world's second-largest exporter of textiles and garments by 2024, trailing only China and outpacing major competitors such as India and Bangladesh (Voice of Vietnam, 2024).

This export dynamism is underpinned by three interrelated pillars: Vietnam's strategic integration into GVCs, competitive labour costs, and favourable trade agreements. First, strategic GVC integration was achieved through Vietnam's proactive engagement with foreign buyers and global brands, beginning in the 1990s, when Japanese and other international investors connected Vietnam to the global garment value chain (Goto, 2023). This integration enabled Vietnamese firms to access advanced production networks, benefit from technology transfer, and secure stable export markets, while facilitating upgrades in the industry's processes, products, and functions.

Second, competitive labour costs have historically given Vietnam a clear comparative advantage, attracting foreign investment and making the country a preferred sourcing destination for global apparel brands. Although average wages in Vietnam have risen in recent years, surpassing those in Bangladesh, Cambodia, and India, the industry has responded by investing in productivity improvements, automation, and digital transformation to sustain competitiveness despite increasing labour costs (Vietnam News, 2024).

Third, favourable trade agreements such as the Comprehensive and Progressive Agreement for Trans–Pacific Partnership (CPTPP) and the EU–Vietnam Free Trade Agreement have expanded Vietnam's access to key markets, such as the EU, Japan, and the US, which together account for more than two-thirds of the country's annual T&C exports (Hoan & Hung, 2024; Nguyen, 2016). These agreements reduce tariffs and incentivise domestic value addition by requiring compliance with strict rules of origin, thus encouraging investment in upstream textile production and supporting sustainable sectoral growth.

Despite its impressive export growth, Vietnam's T&C sector has faced significant import dependency, with export-oriented garment value chains relying heavily on imported yarns and fabrics, with China remaining a major supplier(Goto, 2023; Trần, 2012; Vietnam Textile and Apparel Association, 2023). This structural reliance is rooted in the organisation of the sector within GVCs, where foreign buyers and multinational brands dominate high-value functions such as design, marketing, and sourcing, while Vietnamese manufacturers primarily engage in cut-make-trim and free-on-board production. This hybrid model, typical buyer-driven GVCs, limits domestic firms' opportunities for functional upgrading and backward integration, as most Vietnamese garment enterprises focus on assembly rather than upstream activities, such as spinning, weaving, or dyeing (Goto, 2007, 2023; Hue & Korwatanasakul, 2023). As a result, local value addition remains constrained, and the sector's ability to meet the rules of origin requirements under preferential trade agreements is compromised. To fully benefit from preferential trade agreements such as the CPTPP and the EU–Vietnam Free Trade Agreement, Vietnam's T&C sector must comply with stringent yarn-forward and fabric-forward rules of origin, which require that spinning, weaving, and fabric finishing must be carried out within Vietnam or partner countries rather than rely on imported inputs from non-member countries. Given that domestic fabric production capacity meets only about 20%–30% of demand, and about 60% of textile inputs is imported, with China serving as a major supplier, this import dependent structure directly constrains firms' ability to satisfy these rules and undermines the realisation of tariff preferences that are intended to incentivise upgrading and local value creation (Berger et al., 2016; Bui, 2025; Center for WTO and International Trade – VCCI, 2024).

3.3 Key Challenges for ASEAN's Sustainability

As the previous section traced the evolution of the T&C industries in Cambodia, Myanmar, and Vietnam, it became evident that these countries' integration into GVCs has brought both opportunities and persistent obstacles. Building on that analysis, this section provides an overview of the key challenges for the sustainability of ASEAN's T&C sector. Specifically, we focus on the issues of import dependency, limited domestic linkages, rising wage pressures and technological gaps.

3.3.1 Lack of Vertical Integration: Upstream Bottlenecks and Import Dependency

ASEAN countries remain heavily reliant on imported textiles, notably fabrics and synthetic fibres, despite their dominance in garment assemblies. The trade and GVC indicators presented in Section 3.2 consistently showed high backward participation alongside modest forward participation, indicating that ASEAN competitiveness has been built primarily on downstream assembly that relies on imported yarns, fabrics, and trims rather than on domestic upstream supply (see Section 3.2: Tables 14, 15, and 17 and Figure 5). In the country cases, this dependence is particularly pronounced: Vietnam and Cambodia heavily rely on imported textiles primarily from China, Korea and Taiwan, while Myanmar is a case where over 88% of firms source inputs from abroad, with only 2% reporting local fabric availability (World Bank, 2023).

This pattern is not simply an 'insufficient investment' problem; it is an outcome of the governance structure of buyer-driven apparel value chains (Gereffi et al., 2005). In such chains, lead firms in advanced economies control high-value functions- particularly design, branding and marketing-while production in ASEAN economies is largely confined to lower-value assembly, contributing to persistent upgrading bottlenecks.

3.3.2 Limited Linkages between FDI and Domestic Firms

Despite significant FDI inflows into ASEAN's T&C sector (Figure 6), the spillover effects on domestic firms are limited. Foreign-owned factories often operate as enclaves with minimal technology transfer or knowledge sharing with local suppliers. For example, Cambodia's garment sector employs over 750,000 workers, but its linkage with the domestic economy remained limited, as foreign firms source only 8.2% of their inputs domestically (ASEAN Main Portal, 2024, Winkler, 2022). This disconnect undermines functional upgrading – the shift to higher-value activities, such as design and branding. The limited integration of domestic firms into higher-value activities within GVCs is underpinned by weak institutional frameworks that fail to support supplier development programmes (Dollar & Kidder, 2017; Qiang et al., 2021). Dollar and Kidder (2017) link institutional quality to GVC participation, noting that weaker institutions correlate with reliance on foreign intermediates, as domestic firms cannot produce specialised inputs. Qiang et al. (2021) further emphasise that institutional gaps, such as under-investment in skills training, inadequate infrastructure, and fragmented policies, hinder domestic firms from meeting the compliance and quality standards required for direct exports or higher-value roles. Without targeted interventions such as skills development, financial incentives for domestic input production, and stronger regulatory frameworks, domestic firms will remain marginalised in subcontracting roles and unable to leverage GVC participation for sustainable industrial upgrading.

3.3.3 Wage Increases and Limited Worker Capabilities

Rising wages in ASEAN, particularly in Vietnam (6.3% annually, as shown in Figure 9), threaten cost competitiveness while outpacing productivity gains. Social upgrading – improving wages, working conditions, and skills – is essential for retaining skilled labour and meeting the demands of ethical consumers. World Bank (2022) notes that to maintain export momentum and economic growth, Vietnam and its ASEAN peers must focus on boosting labour productivity by investing in education, workforce skills, and industrial upgrading. Social upgrading-improving wages, working conditions, and workforce skills are recognised as essential for retaining skilled labour and meeting the expectations of increasingly ethical and quality-conscious global consumers (Gama et al., 2018; OECD, 2023b).

Efforts to address these challenges through vocational education and training have yielded inconsistent results. In Vietnam, the Vocational and Technical Education Project, supported by the Asian Development Bank, contributed to improving curriculum methodology and providing modern training equipment in selected vocational institutions (ADB, 2013). However, broader assessments of skill development in Southeast Asia indicate that education and training systems still need to strengthen soft skills such as problem-solving, teamwork, and digital literacy competencies that are increasingly critical for advanced manufacturing and adaptability in a rapidly evolving labour market (OECD, 2021a).

3.3.4 Technological Gaps in SMEs

SMEs dominate ASEAN's T&C sector but struggle to meet the stringent sustainability requirements of global buyers. Many SMEs face the financial, technological constraints in adopting advanced eco-friendly and circular technologies, such as waterless dyeing, closed-loop recycling, or energy-efficient production systems, which require substantial investment in equipment, skills, technology, and supporting infrastructure (ERIA/OECD, 2024; APEC, 2025). In Cambodia and Vietnam, as discussed above in Section 3.3.1, firms-particularly SMEs-that rely heavily on imported fabrics and raw materials struggle to modernise upstream and circular textile activities due to high investment costs, limited access to green finance, weak domestic backward linkages, and insufficient supporting industrial infrastructure, which continue to restrict value-chain upgrading (ASEAN Main Portal, 2024; APEC, 2025).

Institutional weaknesses compound these gaps, including inadequate access to green finance and underdeveloped vocational training programmes. ERIA/OECD (2024) highlights that while regional efforts to promote SME greening are increasing, most SMEs remain in the early stages of adopting sustainable technologies due to limited access to government support, finance, and capacity-building initiatives (ERIA/OECD, 2024; Korwatanasakul & Paweenawat, 2021). This perpetuates reliance on outdated, polluting technologies and underscores the need for more targeted policy interventions, such as subsidised technology transfer programmes and enhanced access to green credit mechanisms, to align SME capabilities with global sustainability standards and ensure equitable participation in green value chains (ERIA/OECD, 2024; OECD, 2021b).

3.4 Industrial Policies

3.4.1 Cambodia

Cambodia's government has implemented targeted policies to reduce import dependency and enhance FDI-domestic linkages in the T&C sector. The Ministry of Economy and Finance's Five-Year Development Plan (2020–2025) aims to increase value addition and productivity in the sector through fiscal incentives, support for domestic textile production, and improved industrial standards (Law on Investment of the Kingdom of Cambodia, 2021). The government also promotes Qualified Investment Project status for export-oriented manufacturers, offering tax holidays of up to nine years and exemptions from import duties on machinery and raw materials, thereby incentivising local sourcing and vertical integration.

Simultaneously, Cambodia promotes joint ventures and technology transfer, as outlined in the Industrial Development Policy 2015–2025, which emphasises SME development and integration into GVCs through the SME Co-Financing Scheme, which provides low-interest loans for technology upgrades (Royal Government of Cambodia, 2015). The Garment, Footwear and Travel Goods Sector Development Strategy 2022–2027 further emphasises skills upgrading, compliance with international labour standards, and improved working conditions, with support from programmes such as the ILO's Better Factories Cambodia (Frederik, 2024). Additionally, the National Roadmap for Sustainable Consumption and Production 2022–2035 guides the sector toward resource efficiency and circular economy practices (GDPS-MOE, 2022).

3.4.2 Myanmar

Myanmar initially showed promise in adopting sustainable T&C policies, but its progress has stalled primarily due to the ongoing political turmoil following the 2021 coup. Pre-coup initiatives, such as the Myanmar Organic Farming Initiative, targeted eco-conscious European markets, promoting organic farming and environmentally sustainable practices (Nordic Development Fund, 2016). The EU-funded SMART Myanmar project further promoted sustainable consumption and production practices, green finance, and gender empowerment in garment factories (EU International Partnerships, 2019). The Thilawa Special Economic Zone (SEZ), operating under the SEZ Law, attracted nearly $2 billion in FDI by 2020, including investment in textile manufacturing facilitated by tax incentives and modern infrastructure (Myanmar Investment Commission, 2020). Social upgrading efforts included the Skills for Employment Program, supported by the ILO, which trained female workers in machine operations and supervisory roles to enhance gender equity in the workforce (ILO, 2018).

However, the February 2021 coup, together with the COVID-19 shock, led to a sharp reversal. Upgrading efforts, including movement beyond the cut-make-pack model and improvements in input sourcing and energy reliability, have remained constrained, leaving the sector vulnerable to power outages, logistics bottlenecks and restrict access to imported inputs. Myanmar's continued reliance on low-value assembly tasks, compounded by political instability, has exacerbated its economic vulnerabilities and reflects a 'survival-oriented', constrained upgrading trajectory (World Bank, 2023).

3.4.3 Vietnam

Vietnam has adopted a systematic and balanced approach to promoting sustainable development in its T&C industry. Central to Vietnam's regulatory framework for the textile and garment sector is Decision No. 1643/QD-TTg (2022), which sets out the 'Strategy for Development of Vietnam's Textiles and Clothing, Leather and Footwear Industries to 2030, with a Vision to 2035'. This strategy prioritises reducing import dependency through localised production, promoting sustainable practices, and integrating circular economic principles (Vietnam Textile and Apparel Association, 2023). Key measures include targeted support for domestic fibre and fabric production, incentives for green industrial parks, and state-backed funding for research and training (Prime Minister of Vietnam, 2022). The Law governs environmental compliance, as outlined in Environmental Protection 2020 and sectoral regulations, such as QCVN 01:2017/BCT and QCVN 13-MT:2015/BTNMT, which establish standards for chemical safety and wastewater discharge (Dang et al., 2024; WWF, 2018). TCVN ISO 26000:2013 and the Law on Enterprises addressed social responsibility and governance. Recent policy initiatives also emphasise circularity, targeting textile waste recycling and traceability (Global Fashion Agenda (GFA), 2024).

3.5 Policy Implications for a Sustainable T&C Value Chain in ASEAN

The T&C sector is fundamental to ASEAN economies, driven by export-oriented growth and integration into GVCs. However, economic inefficiencies, such as import dependency, limited domestic linkages, rising wage pressures and technological gaps have hindered the sustainability of the T&C value chain. Drawing on industrial policies and analyses of key challenges in Vietnam, Cambodia, and Myanmar, this section outlines policy recommendations for promoting sustainable upgrading in the ASEAN T&C sector.

Promoting Vertical Integration for Domestic Value Addition – Gereffi et al. (2005) and subsequent value chain literature emphasise that vertical integration, developing domestic capacity for yarn, fabric, and finishing processes, is critical for value chain upgrading (Barrientos et al., 2011; Gereffi et al., 2005). This enables countries to move beyond low-value assembly, capture greater economic benefits, and reduce their dependency on external suppliers, thereby enhancing competitiveness and resilience.

To address this issue, ASEAN governments must prioritise upstream investments. Vietnam's strategy for developing textiles is a notable example of efforts to localise fabric production and enhance backward linkages (Prime Minister of Vietnam, 2022). As demonstrated by Myanmar's pre-coup organic farming initiatives targeting eco-conscious European markets (Nordic Development Fund, 2016), public–private partnerships can be transformative. Additionally, cluster-based industrial parks integrating raw-material suppliers with garment manufacturers should be established across ASEAN to foster domestic value addition.

Supporting SMEs in Fostering Technological Innovation and Access to Finance – SMEs, which play an important role in ASEAN's T&C sector, face persistent barriers to technological upgrading and access to finance, hindering their ability to compete in increasingly stringent GVCs (Chang et al., 2016; ERIA/OECD, 2024; Korwatanasakul & Paweenawat, 2021). To address these gaps, ASEAN governments should provide targeted subsidies and green financing facilities, such as low-interest loans and credit guarantees, to support SME investments in green technologies, digital transformation, and productivity-enhancing innovation (ERIA/OECD, 2024). Industry 4.0 technologies, as mentioned in the SME Policy Index (ERIA & OECD, 2024), encompass a suite of advanced digital and automation solutions – including artificial intelligence, cybersecurity, digital platforms, cloud computing, and big data analytics – that enable the integration of physical production processes with digital systems to create smart factories and supply chains. These technologies are central to the digital transformation of manufacturing, allowing SMEs to enhance productivity, improve resource efficiency, and respond more flexibly to market demands. By adopting Industry 4.0 solutions, SMEs in the T&C sector can move beyond basic automation to achieve real-time data-driven decision-making, predictive maintenance, and customised production, thereby strengthening their competitiveness in GVCs and supporting the transition toward more sustainable and innovative business models (ERIA & OECD, 2024). Initiatives such as Vietnam's automation grants and Cambodia's credit schemes exemplify effective models, while regional knowledge-sharing platforms and innovation hubs can further scale sustainable practices. Thus, enhanced institutional support is critical for enabling SMEs to drive technological innovation and equitable growth in the T&C sector (World Bank, 2023).

Advancing Social Upgrading through Labour Standards and Skills Development – Social upgrading is crucial for balancing rising wages with productivity improvements in ASEAN's T&C sector. Vietnam's annual wage growth risks undermining cost competitiveness if worker efficiency does not increase proportionately (Vietnam News, 2024). Cambodia has seen improvements in labour compliance through initiatives such as the Better Factories Program, which covers over 703 factories and more than 648,000 workers, contributing to measurable improvements in working conditions and compliance with national and international labour standards (ILO, 2024). However, significant gaps remain in addressing gender disparities; women, who constitute the majority of garment workers, face wage gaps and limited representation in leadership roles (ILO, 2025).

Policymakers should expand vocational training programmes to address these challenges. Vietnam's vocational education and training programme offers technical and managerial training, but it requires the integration of soft skills, such as digital literacy and problem-solving (World Bank, 2021). Targeted gender equity programmes should promote skill development among female workers, enabling them to transition into supervisory roles and leadership positions, thereby aligning with Sustainable Development Goal 5, which focuses on gender equality (ILO, 2025). Furthermore, legislation for living-wage indexes to inflation can help ensure worker welfare while maintaining competitiveness in GVCs.

Promoting Environmental Sustainability and Circular Economy Practices – Environmental sustainability in the ASEAN T&C sector remains underdeveloped. Textile dyeing accounts for 20% of industrial water pollution in major producer countries such as Viet Nam and Myanmar, and the sector struggles to adopt circular economic models (ASEAN Main Portal, 2024; APEC, 2025). Global Standard's Annual Report 2025 suggests that compliance with credible eco-certifications, such as Global Organic Textile Standard, is increasingly important for meeting evolving regulatory requirements, market expectations, and buyer demands, thereby supporting business opportunities in high-value export destinations, including the EU and the US (Global Standard, 2026).

ASEAN policymakers must manage sustainable practices through tax incentives and grants for green technology, primarily at the national level. Targeted fiscal incentives such as Vietnam's Green Credit Fund and Malaysia's Green Investment Tax Allowance have demonstrated effectiveness in accelerating the uptake of energy-efficient and low-carbon technologies, resulting in measurable reductions in operational costs and emissions (MGTC, 2024; PWC, 2025). At the regional level, the ASEAN Secretariat can play a strategic role by facilitating policy dialogues, promoting best practices, and encouraging harmonisation of tax frameworks. By supporting greater access to green finance across the region and fostering regional policy coherence, ASEAN as a whole can foster innovation, enhance global market competitiveness, and ensure a resilient transition toward sustainable industrial development.

3.6 Conclusions

The T&C sector remains a vital yet complex component of ASEAN's economic landscape, characterised by its integration into GVCs and its simultaneous struggle to balance competitiveness and sustainability. This section examines ASEAN countries' participation in T&C GVCs, structural challenges, and policy implications for promoting the sustainability of ASEAN's T&C sector.

The structural challenges facing ASEAN's T&C sector – upstream bottlenecks, weak FDI and local firm linkages, wage pressures, and technological deficits – are deeply interconnected. Vertical integration remains hindered by a dependency on imported textiles, with Cambodia and Vietnam each sourcing approximately 60% of their fabrics externally. This undermines resilience by locking economies into low-value activities, as Kaplinsky and Morris (2002) argued. Meanwhile, rising wages in Vietnam outpace productivity gains, threatening competitiveness without commensurate improvement in workforce skills. These challenges underscore the need for policies harmonising economic growth with social equity and environmental stewardship.

Looking ahead, ASEAN's ability to lead sustainable T&C production hinges on regional cooperation and policy coherence. The ASEAN Circular Economy Framework provides a foundation for harmonising recycling standards and green infrastructure, while trade agreements, such as the Regional Comprehensive Economic Partnership (RCEP) and CPTPP, can facilitate green trade in textile and clothing value chain, could incentivise green tariffs (ASEAN, 2021; Korwatanasakul, 2026). However, evolving EU requirements under the EU Strategy for Sustainable and Circular Textiles on sustainability, circularity, traceability and due diligence, together with buyer expectations for responsible supply chains, necessitate urgent action to avoid compliance risks and maintain access to high-value market (European Commission, 2022; OECD, 2018).

In conclusion, ASEAN stands at a crossroads. By embracing integrated policies that prioritise vertical integration, technological innovation, social equity, and environmental sustainability, the region can transition from a low-cost assembly to a hub of ethical, high-value production. This requires fostering SME capabilities, strengthening regional governance, and aligning industrial strategies with the Sustainable Development Goals. As Humphrey and Schmitz (2002) contend, upgrading in GVCs is not merely economic; it is a holistic process that demands institutional agility and collective action. ASEAN's path to long-term sustainability lies in transcending fragmented approaches and forging a shared vision of inclusive and resilient growth. This includes strengthening institutional capacities, fostering knowledge-sharing mechanisms, and aligning policy objectives to support inclusive growth. A shared regional vision, anchored in principles of resilience, environmental sustainability, and social equity, is essential to address transboundary challenges and leverage collective strengths. Such a coordinated framework enables ASEAN member states to progress collectively in the GVC hierarchy while ensuring that economic upgrading does not exacerbate inequality or environmental degradation.

4 Automobile

4.1 Introduction

The automobile industry has emerged as a significant growth engine within ASEAN, contributing significantly to the region's economic development. In 2020, the sector was estimated to add at least $177 billion to ASEAN's GDP, representing approximately 6.3% of the region's total GDP (Korwatanasakul & Intarakumnerd, 2020). Beyond its direct economic contribution, the industry is also a vital source of employment, supporting over 2.4 million jobs across ASEAN.

ASEAN has established itself as a crucial production base for the global automotive industry. The industry encompasses a wide range of vehicles, including passenger cars, motorcycles, trucks, and related parts and components. Among the region's manufacturing sectors, the automotive industry ranks among the largest and most dynamic.

This section defines the automobile industry in a narrower sense, focusing specifically on passenger vehicles (cars) and their associated parts and components. While the broader automotive industry includes a variety of motorised vehicles – such as buses, motorcycles, off-road vehicles, and trucks – the analysis in this section focuses primarily on the car sector. Nevertheless, given the differences in industrial classifications across datasets, both broader and narrower definitions of the industry are occasionally used, depending on the

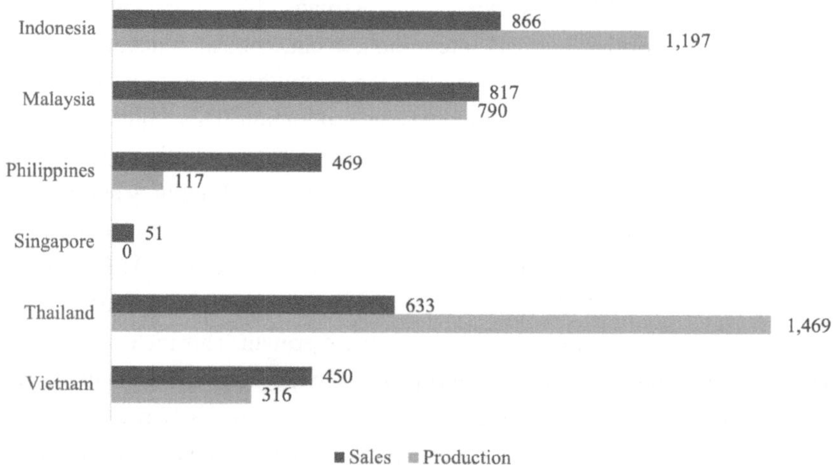

Figure 10 ASEAN: Motor vehicle sales and production, 2024 (Thousands of units).

Source: Authors, based on Marklines, Macroeconomic statistics from Fitch, PwC Research and Analysis ASEAN-6 Automotive Market Snapshot.

data source. To ensure a comprehensive and consistent examination of the automobile industry, three primary data sources are employed: the AJC-UNCTAD-Eora database on ASEAN GVCs, the Organisation for Economic Cooperation and Development (OECD) Input–Output Tables, and the UN Comtrade Database. Efforts were made to harmonise these datasets to best capture the industry's dynamics, although some discrepancies across countries and data sources persist.

According to Figure 10, ASEAN countries produced approximately 4.4 million vehicles, catering to both domestic and international markets. Thailand led the region, with production reaching approximately 1.47 million units, followed by Indonesia with around 1.2 million units. Malaysia produced around 790,000 vehicles, positioning itself as another crucial automotive hub. Meanwhile, Vietnam and the Philippines recorded production of 316,000 and 117,000 vehicles, respectively, while Singapore reported no significant production.

Sales figures reveal different market dynamics. Indonesia recorded the highest domestic vehicle sales at around 866,000 units, followed by Malaysia with 817,000 units. Thailand's domestic sales reached about 633,000 units, while the Philippines and Vietnam showed growing markets with sales of 469,000 and 450,000 units, respectively. Despite lacking domestic production, Singapore reported sales of about 51,000 units, reflecting continued consumer demand.

These figures highlight Thailand's strong position as ASEAN's leading production hub, heavily oriented toward exports, while Indonesia demonstrates a balance between large-scale production and robust domestic consumption. Malaysia maintains a relatively even balance between production and sales, indicating a more domestically driven industry. In contrast, the Philippines and Vietnam exhibit a pattern where domestic demand exceeds domestic production, necessitating significant imports.

Exports further emphasise the industry's importance to the region's economy. In 2017, ASEAN's finished automobile exports were valued at $14.5 billion, while total exports from the broader automotive sector – including parts and components – reached $51 billion, accounting for roughly 4% of ASEAN's total export value (Korwatanasakul & Intarakumnerd, 2020).

On the global stage, ASEAN producers performed competitively: Thailand ranked 10th worldwide in 2024, followed by Indonesia (14th), Malaysia (19th), Vietnam (32nd), the Philippines (35th), and Myanmar (44th).[6] These rankings reflect ASEAN's increasingly important role in the global automotive value chain and integration into international production networks.

4.2 Structure and Global Value Chain Integration of the ASEAN Automobile Industry

4.2.1 Structure of the ASEAN Automobile Industry

Despite its complexity and multilayered structure, the automobile industry has become deeply integrated into RVCs and GVCs through international production fragmentation. As an essentially assembly-based industry, it encompasses a sophisticated network of assemblers and suppliers that manufacture a vast array of parts and components. These range from simple, labour-intensive products, such as seat covers, to highly complex, capital-intensive systems, like electronic modules.

The production system in the automobile sector is organised vertically, with parts and components sequentially manufactured and transferred from upstream to downstream stages. Although automotive parts are often produced and assembled across different countries, production activities tend to cluster geographically in specialised industrial hubs. ASEAN suppliers, in particular, are closely linked to regional and global production networks dominated by major global car manufacturers, notably Japanese firms.

Since the 1990s, the GVC concept has been widely used to explain the highly fragmented and globally integrated nature of automotive production. Outsourcing

[6] International Organization of Motor Vehicle Manufacturer: www.oica.net/category/production-statistics/2024-statistics/.

and offshoring strategies have allowed firms to capitalise on the international division of labour and specialisation. R&D, design, and engineering are typically retained in the home countries of lead firms, while final assembly operations are located in markets with strong domestic demand, such as Indonesia, or in markets with strategic export advantages, such as Thailand. Bulky and model-specific components are often produced near assembly plants to minimise logistics costs and maximise production efficiency through just-in-time inventory systems (Sturgeon et al., 2016). Conversely, lighter, more standardised parts are outsourced to countries with lower labour costs.

This pattern of geographically concentrated production within regional systems, often referred to as 'build-where-they-sell' strategies (Dowlah, 2018), highlights the importance of regionalisation even within globally connected value chains. Despite the global footprint of lead firms and Tier-1 suppliers, a substantial degree of localisation remains essential for operational efficiency (OECD, 2012). Specific segments of production, particularly those requiring tacit knowledge, are tightly clustered in global automotive hubs such as Detroit (US), Toyota City (Japan), and Stuttgart (Germany) (Korwatanasakul & Intarakumnerd, 2020).

The organisational structure of the automobile GVC can be conceptualised through a tier system, as shown in Table 18. At the apex are the assemblers and OEMs, typically large MNCs such as Toyota, Ford, and General Motors. These firms control the industry's most capital- and technology-intensive segments, including core technologies, R&D, product design, marketing, and final vehicle assembly.

Tier-1 suppliers, often referred to as module and system integrators, closely collaborate with OEMs. Many of these Tier-1 suppliers are mega-suppliers – large multinational firms or subsidiaries of OEMs such as Denso (a Toyota spin-off) – and are known for 'follow sourcing', relocating operations to stay close to their main assembler clients (Natsuda & Thoburn, 2018). These suppliers specialise in integrating components into modules, such as cockpit assemblies or chassis systems, and act as critical 'gatekeepers' in the GVC, influencing the access of lower-tier suppliers (Dowlah, 2018). Modules represent key building blocks within the production structure, comprising systems such as the interior system (e.g., seats and dashboards), body system (e.g., doors and trim), chassis system (e.g., drive shafts and suspension modules), and electrical and electronic systems (e.g., vehicle electronics and wiring) (Sturgeon et al., 2016).

As the industry's technological demands increased, Tier-0.5 suppliers emerged to share the responsibilities of Tier-1 suppliers. While the distinction between Tier-0.5 and Tier-1 suppliers can be ambiguous, Tier-0.5 suppliers are typically more involved in design and development activities, supporting

Table 18 Structure of the automobile industry and GVC participation.

Tiers	OEM	Tier-3	Tier-3	Tier-2	Tier-1	Tier-0.5	OEM	OEM
Players	Standardisers (OEMs)	Raw material suppliers	Engineering material and special services suppliers	Component specialists	Module and system Integrators (Mega-suppliers)	Module and system Integrators (Mega-suppliers)	Assemblers (OEMs)	Distributors and exporters
Function	R&D & design	Material supply (upstream industry)	Engineering material and special services supply	Parts and components sourcing	Module and system integration	Design and develop modules, auto parts and systems	Assembling	Marketing, distribution and after-sales services
Products	Technology and product design	Steel, rubber, electronics, plastic, glass, and textile	Brake fluid and antifreeze	Auto parts and components	Interior system, body system, chassis system, and electrical and electronic system	Interior system, body system, chassis system, and electrical and electronic system	Automobiles (final product)	N/A

Table 18 (cont.)

Tiers	OEM	Tier-3	Tier-3	Tier-2	Tier-1	Tier-0.5	OEM	OEM
Costs	Low to medium	Low	Low	High	High	High	Low	Medium - High
Producer countries	China, Europe, Japan, Korea (the Republic of), and the US	Australia, China, Europe, India, Indonesia, Japan, Korea (the Republic of), Malaysia, Thailand and the US	Australia, China, Europe, India, Indonesia, Japan, Korea (the Republic of), Malaysia, Thailand and the US	Cambodia, Indonesia, the Lao PDR, Malaysia, Myanmar, the Philippines, Thailand, and Vietnam	Indonesia, Malaysia, the Philippines, Thailand, and Vietnam	Indonesia, Malaysia, the Philippines, Thailand, and Vietnam	Brunei Darussalam, Cambodia, Indonesia, Malaysia, Myanmar, the Philippines, Thailand, and Vietnam	N/A
GVC participation	High	Low	Low	Low	Medium - High	Medium - High	High	N/A

Source: Authors, based on Korwatanasakul and Intarakumnerd (2020)

Note: Lao PDR = Lao People's Democratic Republic, OEM = original equipment manufacturers, R&D = research and design, US = United States

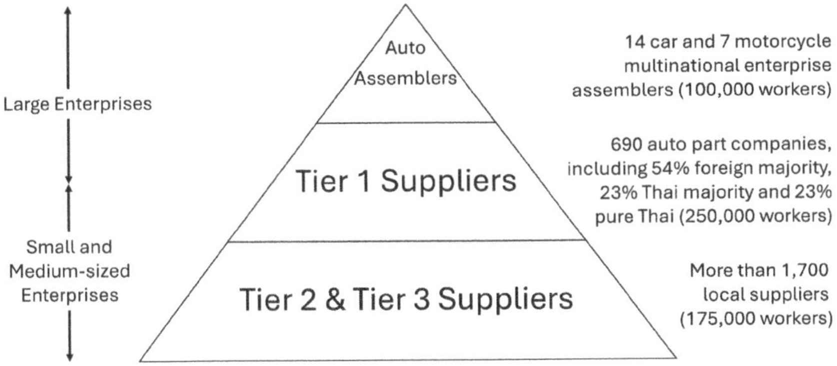

Figure 11 Structure of the Thai Automotive Industry, 2018.

Source: Korwatanasakul and Intarakumnerd (2020).

assemblers beyond mere manufacturing by contributing to product innovation. Tier-2 suppliers primarily produce auto parts and components that Tier-1 firms integrate into modules and systems. Tier-3 suppliers provide raw materials and basic industrial inputs – such as rubber, plastics, textiles, and metals – that are fundamental for automotive manufacturing but relatively low in technological intensity. All suppliers in Tier-2 and Tier-3 are local firms.

For instance, although local Thai suppliers are compelled to enhance their processes and adopt better technologies to comply with international standards and maintain their position in the value chain, their activities remain concentrated in lower-tier segments with limited technological complexity. As of 2018, Thailand's automotive sector comprised over 2,400 firms, with approximately 1,700 domestic Tier-2 and Tier-3 suppliers and around 690 Tier-1 suppliers – owned by a mix of foreign and local stakeholders (Figure 11). In contrast, vehicle assembly operations were entirely controlled by MNCs, consisting of fourteen car and seven motorcycle assemblers. Consequently, the DVA in Thailand's automotive exports is primarily derived from labour inputs and the competitive advantage of low-cost assembly rather than from domestically developed technologies. This underscores the critical role of DVA quality, where labour-based advantages dominate over technological capabilities, in shaping industrial and economic development outcomes.

Participation in the automobile GVC varies across ASEAN member states (Table 18). Thailand and Indonesia serve as regional production hubs for global carmakers, supported by strong manufacturing bases and sizeable domestic markets. Malaysia occupies a mid-tier position with moderate production capacity. Meanwhile, the Philippines and Vietnam primarily concentrate on completely knocked-down assembly and the production of specific parts, such as wiring harnesses and electronic components. Cambodia and Myanmar engage mainly in completely built-up production through completely knocked-down kits, while the Lao PDR has minimal involvement in automobile assembly.[7] Cambodia, the Lao PDR, and Myanmar (collectively known as CLM countries) have benefited from the 'China-Plus-One' and 'Thailand-Plus-One' strategies, which relocated Tier-2 supplier activities to lower-cost environments. While lacking primary vehicle production, Singapore specialises in high-value activities such as automotive electronics, regional distribution, and emerging areas like autonomous vehicle development. Brunei Darussalam has recently developed an electric vehicle assembly plant, signalling a new entry into the regional GVC.

The automobile GVC is continuously evolving, driven by advances in technology and innovation. On the production side, multinational mega-suppliers and Tier-0.5 firms are playing increasingly prominent roles, while OEMs are adopting global platform strategies to reduce costs and achieve economies of scale. On the product development side, ASEAN countries increasingly emphasise green technologies (Keawsuwan, 2015). Indonesia promotes its low-cost green car programme, Malaysia seeks to position itself as a hub for energy-efficient vehicles, and Thailand aims to become a global hub for green automotive manufacturing. The Philippines has introduced incentives for electric and hybrid vehicles, and even Brunei Darussalam has entered the field by investing in green automotive manufacturing. These emerging trends are expected to reshape the structure and dynamics of the automobile GVCs in ASEAN and beyond, with green technology and innovation becoming central pillars of future industry development.

4.2.2 Value Added and Output of the ASEAN Automobile Industry

Although ASEAN's automobile sector has experienced significant growth, it remains characterised by limited value addition and multiplier effects compared to broader industrial averages. Nevertheless, differences in value-added content and GVC positioning reveal distinct patterns among ASEAN member states. These variations reflect divergent industrial policies, levels of domestic supplier development, and the extent of integration into upstream and downstream segments of global production networks.

The ASEAN automobile industry is concentrated mainly in auto parts manufacturing and final assembly, situating the region's activities predominantly in

[7] Completely knocked-down: Products are imported as disassembled parts and assembled locally, involving limited local value addition mainly through assembly.

Completely built-up: Products are imported as fully assembled finished goods, with little or no local production involved.

Table 19 Value added and output of motor vehicles, trailers and semi-trailers compared with all industries, 2015 (Millions of dollars and %).

A. Motor vehicles, trailers and semi-trailers

	Value added	Output	Ratio of value added to output
Brunei Darussalam	65	164	0.40
Cambodia	193	458	0.42
Indonesia	15,735	34,511	0.46
Malaysia	1,438	12,133	0.12
Philippines	2,940	8,759	0.34
Singapore	710	1,848	0.38
Thailand	7,844	36,634	0.21
Vietnam	2,271	10,610	0.21
ASEAN total	31,196	105,117	0.30

B. All industries

	Value added	Output	Ratio of value added to output
Brunei Darussalam	13,174	22,921	0.57
Cambodia	16,984	30,075	0.56
Indonesia	833,734	1,635,254	0.51
Malaysia	292,523	763,255	0.38
Philippines	286,120	555,126	0.52
Singapore	275,238	770,936	0.36
Thailand	378,162	917,981	0.41
Vietnam	175,692	570,060	0.31
ASEAN total	2,271,627	5,265,608	0.43

Source: Authors, based on OECD Input–Output table database.

the middle and downstream stages of the GVC. These segments tend to be labour-intensive and less technologically sophisticated, contributing to limited domestic value generation. As illustrated in Table 19, the ASEAN average ratio of value added to output in the motor vehicle industry was 0.30 in 2015, significantly below the all-industry average of 0.43. Malaysia, Thailand, Vietnam, and the Philippines reported particularly low value-added ratios, reflecting their reliance on imported components and limited local innovation or proprietary technologies.

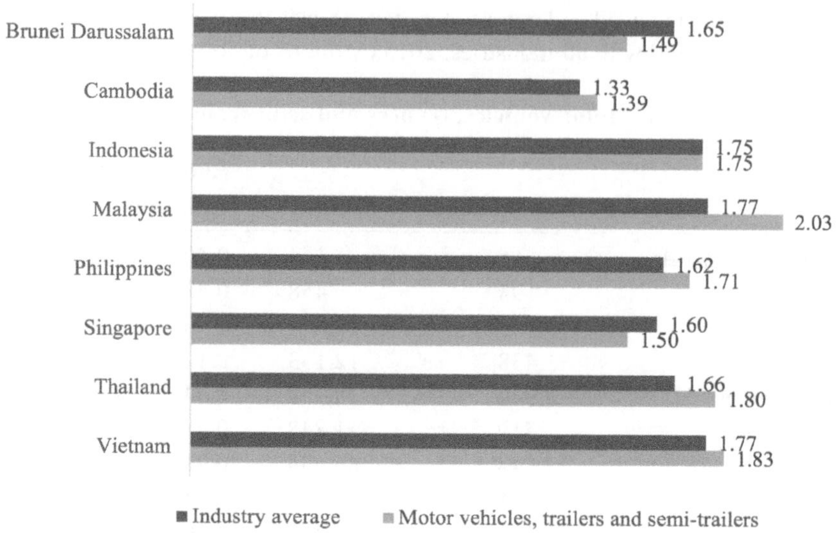

Figure 12 Multiplier effects of motor vehicles, trailers and semi-trailers compared with the industry average, 2015.

Source: Authors, based on OECD Input–Output table database.

Although the automobile sector is linked to a broad set of upstream and downstream industries, its multiplier effects remain relatively weak. As shown in Figure 12, every additional dollar of final demand for motor vehicles generates, on average, $1.69 in additional output across domestic industries. While Malaysia stands out with a multiplier effect of 2.03, other ASEAN economies either perform slightly below or near the regional average. The limited domestic multiplier stems from heavy reliance on foreign inputs in final assembly and the upstream positioning of some economies (e.g. raw materials and parts supply), where demand does not stimulate downstream sectors effectively (Korwatanasakul & Intarakumnerd, 2020).

Figure 13 highlights changes in value-added trade over time. From 1990 to 2015, ASEAN's DVA in exports increased from 43% to 56%, while FVA declined from 57% to 44%. This shift occurred alongside a sharp rise in gross exports, which grew by 10% annually, and a nearly seventeen-fold increase in the volume of DVA. These improvements reflect stronger local sourcing and productivity gains by domestic firms in some ASEAN countries.

Despite the region's dependence on foreign inputs, GVC upgrading has occurred in specific contexts. Figure 14 reveals notable variation across countries in the domestic and foreign value-added composition of automotive exports. Myanmar and Indonesia, for example, exhibit very high domestic

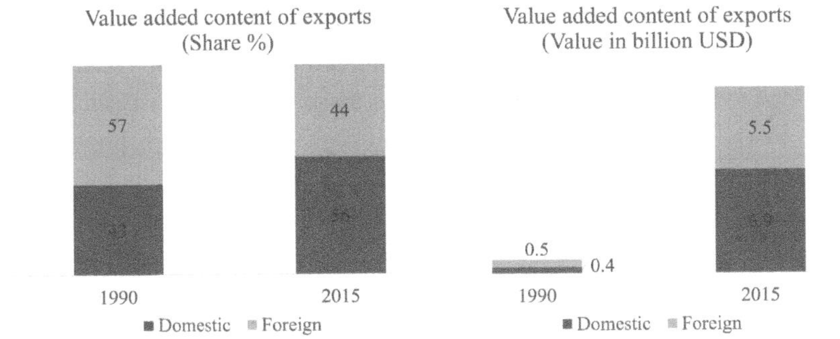

Figure 13 Value added content of exports (% and billions of dollars).
Source: Authors, based on UNCTAD-EORA database.

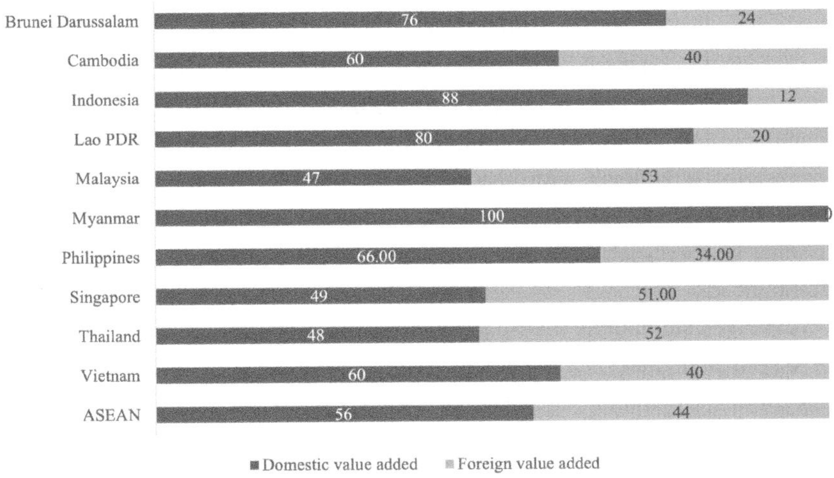

Figure 14 Share of domestic and foreign value added in the automobile industry, 2015 (%).
Source: Authors, based on UNCTAD-Eora database.

content (100% and 88%, respectively), indicating greater concentration in upstream, input-providing activities. In contrast, Malaysia and Thailand, which specialise in advanced manufacturing and final assembly, exhibit higher foreign content – 53% and 52%, respectively – implying stronger reliance on imported technologies and components. Yet Thailand manages to convert this into substantial export value (over $4.3 billion in 2015), whereas Malaysia struggles to do so, likely due to its focus on national car projects that serve the domestic market and are less integrated into international production networks.

The interpretation of these value-added patterns aligns with the notion of GVC positioning. Countries situated upstream, primarily providing materials or parts, tend to have higher DVA shares, while those located downstream, focusing on final assembly or processing, exhibit higher FVA shares. Importantly, GVC participation provides a more balanced view of integration by accounting for the dual roles countries play – as both users and providers of value in multistage global production. However, an exclusive focus on increasing DVA may overlook the strategic value of downstream activities, which can deliver significant development gains, such as employment, market access, and exposure to foreign technologies. In addition, as a high level of DVA does not guarantee economic and social benefits, it is essential to understand contextual, industry-specific value chain components – particularly the quality of DVA sources, including factors such as labour cost advantages and domestic innovation capacity (Korwatanasakul, 2023a).

Overall, the relatively high DVA shares across ASEAN indicate that while the automobile sector is globally integrated, many activities – especially in parts manufacturing – remain localised within domestic industrial clusters. This localisation, combined with historical local content requirements policies in the 1970s, explains the industry's relatively strong domestic linkages compared to other sectors, such as electronics, where GVC fragmentation is much more pronounced.

ASEAN's automobile industry has increased its economic footprint in terms of output and trade, but continues to face challenges in value capture and integration. Upgrading participation in GVCs will require targeted strategies, such as enhancing local supplier capabilities, promoting innovation, and fostering deeper integration with regional and global partners. Leveraging value-added trade indicators can help policymakers and industry leaders diagnose bottlenecks and identify opportunities for structural transformation.

4.2.3 Regional Value Chains of the ASEAN Automobile Industry

FVA plays a critical role in shaping the export structure of ASEAN's automobile industry. As shown in Figure 15, Japan, China, and the US are the top three contributors of foreign inputs incorporated into ASEAN automobile exports, accounting for $898 million (16.3%), $864 million (15.7%), and $424 million (8%), respectively, in 2015. These three countries, especially Japan, have long-established production and technology linkages with Southeast Asia, particularly through Japanese automakers and their regional supplier networks.

Japan's leading role reflects the dominance of Japanese carmakers and Tier-1 suppliers in ASEAN's automotive landscape, underpinned by long-standing

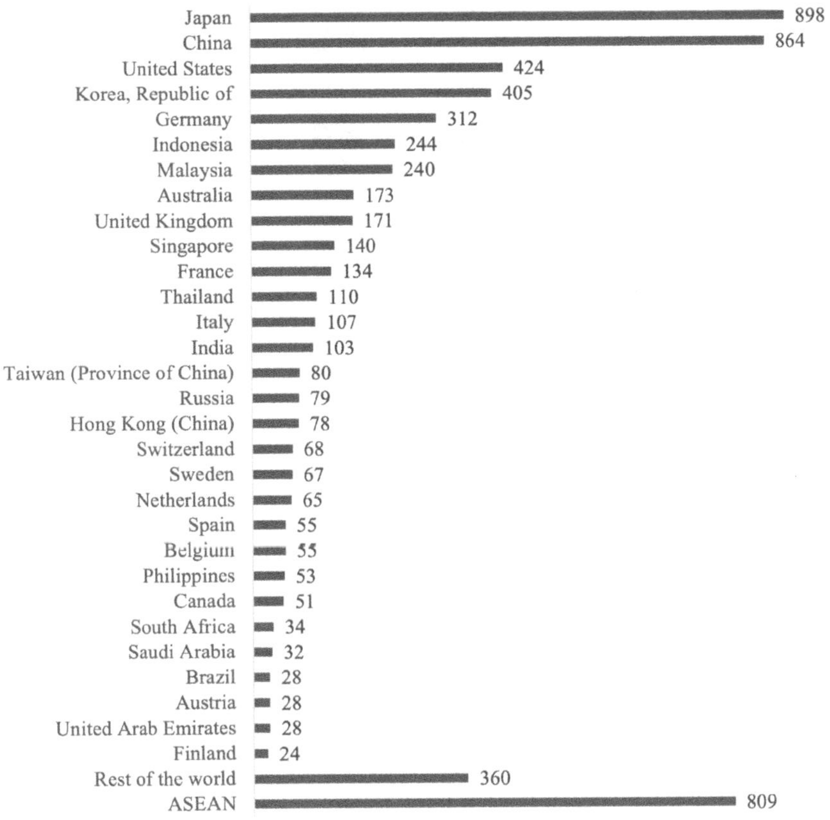

Figure 15 Top thirty foreign value-added creators for ASEAN's automobile industry exports, 2015 (Millions of dollars).

Source: Authors, based on UNCTAD-Eora database.

Japanese FDI that has anchored regional production networks and enabled technology transfer and supplier upgrading. Joint ventures and sustained relationships with Japanese firms – such as Perodua with Daihatsu and the regional manufacturing and R&D operations of Honda – have supported the development of local capabilities, even as core automotive technologies remain concentrated in Japan (Korwatanasakul & Intarakumnerd, 2020).[8] Proximity, established logistics channels, and efficiency in supply chain management further contribute to Japan's continued relevance, even as its relative share declines. China's rising contribution reflects its emergence as a major global manufacturing hub, deeper integration with Southeast Asia, and cost

[8] For a detailed discussion of Japanese FDI and firm-level upgrading in ASEAN's automobile industry, see the case studies in Korwatanasakul and Intarakumnerd (2020).

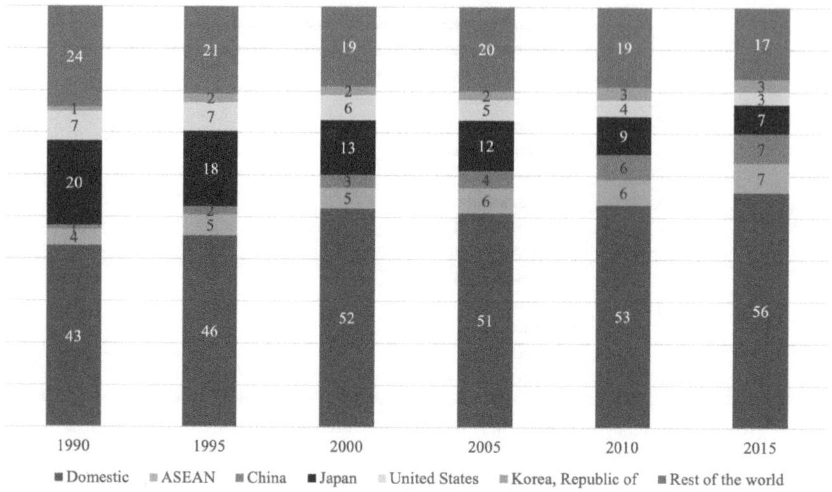

Figure 16 Value added exports of the automobile industry from ASEAN by domestic, ASEAN and other top-four foreign country value-added creators, selected years (%).

Source: Authors, based on UNCTAD-Eora database.

competitiveness, while the US ranks third, mainly due to exports of technology-intensive components to ASEAN markets.

Intra-ASEAN trade has become a significant source of FVA to the region's automotive exports. In 2015, inputs sourced from other ASEAN countries totalled $809 million, accounting for 15 % of total FVA – surpassing the contribution of the US. Indonesia, Malaysia, and Singapore are ranked among the top ten FVA contributors, while the Philippines and Thailand also appear in the top thirty (Figure 15). This highlights the emergence of ASEAN as a regional production hub under the 'Factory Asia' model, where parts, modules, and subassemblies are traded within the region before being exported in their final form.

The evolution of FVA contributors over time is visualised in Figure 16, which tracks the share of value-added exports from ASEAN's automobile industry by source. From 1990 to 2015, the shares of Japan and the US steadily declined, while those of China and ASEAN countries rose. This shift reflects structural changes – such as the relocation of Japanese and US production facilities to ASEAN due to trade liberalisation – and policy-driven regional integration, which encouraged sourcing within ASEAN.

Alongside these compositional shifts, ASEAN's value chain participation has also evolved. Table 20 illustrates trends in both GVC and RVC participation from 1990 to 2015. Overall, GVC participation – defined as the sum of FVA and

Table 20 GVC and RVC participation in automobile industry exports, 1990–2015 (% of total exports).

A. Foreign value added (FVA)

Year	Total	Outside ASEAN	Within ASEAN
1990	56.7	53.2	3.5
1995	53.6	48.6	5.0
2000	48.4	43.2	5.2
2005	48.9	43.0	5.9
2010	47.1	40.7	6.4
2015	44.3	37.8	6.5

B. Domestic value added incorporated in other countries' exports (DVX)

Year	Total	Outside ASEAN	Within ASEAN
1990	13.3	10.9	2.4
1995	12.3	8.8	3.5
2000	13.1	9.2	3.9
2005	13.6	9.6	4.0
2010	15.5	10.7	4.8
2015	15.5	10.5	5.0

C. Value chain participation

Year	Global	Regional
1990	70.0	5.9
1995	65.9	8.5
2000	61.5	9.1
2005	62.5	9.9
2010	62.6	11.2
2015	59.8	11.5

Source: Authors, based on UNCTAD-Eora database.

DVX – declined from 70% in 1990 to 59.8% in 2015. This reduction is primarily due to the declining share of FVA generated outside ASEAN, which decreased from 53.2% to 37.8% during this period.

In contrast, RVC participation – which accounts for FVA and DVX created within ASEAN – has increased steadily, rising from 5.9% to 11.5%. This suggests that ASEAN countries are not only importing and assembling parts but are also increasingly contributing to each other's exports, primarily through the production of intermediate goods and parts. In particular, the rise in DVX incorporated within ASEAN (from 2.4% to 5.0%) highlights the deepening of forward linkages in regional production.

This structural shift reflects the growing importance of ASEAN as a regional value-adding hub supported by integrated supply chains, transport infrastructure, and harmonised standards. Foreign automakers have increasingly located production bases in ASEAN not only to serve domestic markets but also to facilitate regional and global exports. As a result, the share of foreign inputs sourced from outside ASEAN has declined, while intraregional sourcing has expanded, leading to stronger regional production networks.

ASEAN's automobile value chains are transitioning from global dependence to regional resilience. With the deepening of intraregional trade, growing domestic capacity, and an increasing policy focus on integration and innovation, the region is well-positioned to enhance its role not only as a production base but also as a value creator in the global automotive industry.

4.3 Global Value Chain Integration of the ASEAN Automobile Industry – Country-Level Analysis

ASEAN member states exhibit diverse patterns of engagement in the automotive GVC, shaped by differences in market size, industrial policy, institutional capacity, and regional positioning. While some countries, like Indonesia and Thailand, have developed robust domestic industries with high levels of foreign investment and export activity, others remain at the early stages of integration or focus primarily on low-skill, labour-intensive segments. This section presents a country-by-country analysis, highlighting the specific trajectories, structural constraints, and opportunities for upgrading across ASEAN's automotive sectors.

4.3.1 Brunei Darussalam

Brunei Darussalam remains the only ASEAN member state that is not actively engaged in the automotive GVC. The country's economic structure relies heavily on oil and gas, and with a small population and declining birth rates, national development strategies have prioritised less labour-intensive sectors. Automotive manufacturing is not currently included among Brunei Darussalam's five key business clusters – halal products, technology and creative industries, business services, tourism, and downstream oil and gas – and there is no overarching national policy for the automotive industry. Nonetheless, in 2016, Brunei Darussalam made a preliminary move toward entering the sector by signing a memorandum of understanding with China's Shenglong Energy Automobile to explore the establishment of a manufacturing and assembly facility for electric and renewable energy-powered vehicles. While still in the conceptual phase, this initiative reflects a potential shift in Brunei Darussalam's diversification strategy, aligning with global trends toward green and sustainable mobility.

4.3.2 Cambodia

Cambodia's automobile industry remains in its nascent stage but has the potential to strengthen its industrial base by leveraging its role in ASEAN's regional production networks and its strategic position under the Greater Mekong Subregion cooperation and the Thailand-plus-one strategy. Japanese-led production fragmentation and regional expansion have led several major automakers from Thailand and Vietnam to extend lower-tier supplier networks into Cambodia, attracted by competitive labour costs (Tongurai & Fujioka 2017). While most of Cambodia's activity involves completely built-up assembly using completely knocked-down kits, FDI has been limited to a few OEMs, such as Ford (via RMA Group), Hyundai-LYP, and BAIC-Khmer First Car. These firms benefit from SEZs and their geographic proximity to established automotive hubs.

Despite growing gross exports and participation in GVCs, the auto parts industry remains underdeveloped and heavily reliant on imported inputs. Although DVA slightly exceeds FVA, this is primarily due to labour-intensive production rather than robust capacity. The industry is currently dominated by Japanese firms, including Denso, Yazaki, and Toyota Tsusho, which produce wiring systems, castings, motors, and seat covers (DiCaprio & Suvannaphakdy, 2017). Key challenges include rising wages without corresponding productivity gains, labour shortages and turnover, limited human capital, and regulatory opacity. Cambodia must move beyond cost advantages and invest in workforce development, local supplier upgrading, and improved institutional transparency to sustain competitiveness and attract higher-value investments.

4.3.3 Indonesia

Indonesia has emerged as a key player in ASEAN's automotive industry, primarily driven by its large domestic market and growing investment from Japanese automakers. Although most vehicles produced are sold domestically, the country holds the second-highest DVA share in automotive exports among ASEAN countries, attributed mainly to the export of parts and components rather than complete vehicles. The automotive sector contributes significantly to Indonesia's economy, accounting for approximately 10% of the GDP and employing hundreds of thousands of workers (Kaiser, 2018). With West Java, notably Bekasi, serving as the central industrial hub, the country's automotive ecosystem comprises over 1,500 firms. However, technological upgrading remains a challenge. Most domestic suppliers are in Tier-2 or Tier-3, producing specific components with limited potential to advance up the value chain due to their low technological capacity and reliance on imported parts. While joint ventures with foreign OEMs like Toyota and Mitsubishi help transfer some production capabilities, local firms remain passive learners and lack strong innovation systems or institutional support (Korwatanasakul & Intarakumnerd, 2020).

Indonesia's automotive policy shifted from protectionist approaches in the 1970s, including import substitution and national car projects, to liberalisation following the 1997 Asian financial crisis. Although the country has attracted significant foreign investment, efforts to develop indigenous automotive technology have lagged. Government initiatives, such as the low-cost green car programme, have driven recent growth, especially in multipurpose vehicles. Despite the high DVA share, about 70 % of parts for domestic automobile production are still imported, and export figures are concentrated in parts and components rather than finished vehicles. More structured university-industry linkages, institutionalised collaboration with foreign firms, and stronger support for local firms to meet international standards are necessary to achieve sustainable upgrading (Intarakumnerd, 2011).

4.3.4 The Lao PDR

The Lao PDR is among the least developed participants in ASEAN's automotive value chain, primarily supplying low-cost labour under the Greater Mekong Subregion Economic Cooperation and the Thailand-plus-one strategy. The country lacks completely knocked-down assembly facilities and remains a net importer of vehicles. However, in recent years, MNCs – such as Toyota Boshoku and Asahi Tec – have set up labour-intensive component manufacturing operations, particularly in the Savan-Seno SEZ. These firms, along with others like Yazaki and Suzuki, benefit from proximity to Thailand and Vietnam, using the Lao PDR as a base for producing components such as seat covers and aluminium die-cast parts.

While total exports from the Lao PDR's automotive parts and components industry remain modest, they have increased sharply since 2000, especially in terms of DVA. This DVA share stems mainly from labour-intensive production rather than local technological capability. Foreign value added remains relatively low, indicating limited dependence on imported intermediate goods. However, this model leaves the Lao PDR vulnerable, as its competitiveness hinges on maintaining low wages. Rising labour costs, limited human capital, and high turnover rates pose long-term challenges. The country lacks a dedicated automotive policy but has general investment laws and SEZ regulations supporting industrial development. Labour force development is a stated priority, but no specific strategies for technological upgrading in the automotive sector have been implemented.

4.3.5 Malaysia

Malaysia's automotive industry is primarily shaped by its national car projects – Proton and Perodua – which once aimed to foster indigenous technological capabilities and strengthen local suppliers. These firms dominate the domestic passenger car market, giving Malaysia the highest share of national brands in ASEAN. The sector contributes approximately 4% of GDP and generates up to 700,000 jobs, including indirect employment (Ministry of International Trade and Industry, Malaysia, 2017). However, despite producing over 4,000 automotive components, 86 % of sales are concentrated in the local market, and Malaysia's DVA share remains relatively low. National carmakers, long protected by government policies, have struggled to compete internationally due to limited global integration and innovation capacity. Similarly, local suppliers – often protected under the New Economic Policy – lag behind their regional peers in terms of competitiveness, pricing, and technological advancement.

Since the 1970s, the Malaysian government has actively shaped the automotive industry through industrial policy, tariff protection, and regulatory incentives. The launch of Proton in 1985, in collaboration with Mitsubishi, and Perodua in 1993, catalysed the development of local supplier networks. However, trade liberalisation under the ASEAN Free Trade Area (AFTA) has significantly reduced import tariffs, exposing the domestic industry to foreign competition. While Proton and Perodua engage in full-cycle design and manufacturing, most parts suppliers remain focused on low-tech components and exhibit limited innovation. Some firms – especially those linked with MNCs – have developed export capacity and technological capabilities, but these are exceptions rather than the norm.

To advance in GVCs, Malaysia must foster stronger linkages between local suppliers and MNCs, alongside enhanced support for R&D and technological upgrading (Intarakumnerd, 2011). Foreign assemblers have well-developed intra-firm networks but rarely facilitate spillovers to local firms. The small size of the domestic market and slow product life cycles further reduce incentives to innovate. Nonetheless, firms that have proactively built relationships with MNCs or accessed export markets through internal capability development demonstrate that upgrading is possible. These cases underline the importance of targeted policies that promote collaborative innovation, supplier upgrading, and deeper integration into advanced production networks.

4.3.6 Myanmar

Myanmar's automotive industry is in its early stages of development but holds potential for greater integration into GVCs, driven by its abundant low-cost labour, natural resources, and strategic location between India and China. Since opening up in 2012, Myanmar has attracted foreign automakers, including Suzuki, Toyota, Nissan, Hyundai, and Ford, which have established completely knocked-down-based assembly lines in the Thilawa SEZ and the Yangon area. However, the country still relies heavily on used-car imports to meet domestic demand, undermining economies of scale and hindering the development of a robust domestic automotive and auto parts industry. While there has been investment in labour-intensive component production – such as tyres, wiper system hoses, and small motors – productivity challenges, inadequate infrastructure, and limited support services remain key obstacles. Myanmar's relatively high DVA share in exports is primarily attributed to low wages rather than advanced local capabilities.

Despite these constraints, Myanmar has engaged in policy dialogue, particularly with Japan, to promote the development of its automotive sector. In 2013, a joint initiative between Myanmar's Ministry of Planning and Finance and Japanese organisations, such as the Japan External Trade Organization, emphasised support for SMEs, the development of new car markets, and the potential establishment of an automotive recycling system (JETRO, 2018). The proposed recycling initiative presents an opportunity for functional upgrading and a first-mover advantage within the region. To become a future hub in the automobile industry, Myanmar must overcome stiff competition from regional leaders such as Thailand, Indonesia, and China while addressing its domestic challenges in productivity, infrastructure, and institutional capacity. These efforts, however, have been significantly disrupted by the ongoing political crisis since the 2021 military coup. Political instability, international sanctions, and a deteriorating business climate have severely constrained foreign investment, disrupted industrial activities, and undermined investor confidence. As a result, progress on automotive policy and sectoral upgrading remains uncertain in the current context.

4.3.7 The Philippines

The Philippines' participation in the GVC is primarily focused on the production of auto parts and components rather than complete vehicle assembly. Due to a small domestic market, local assemblers struggle to achieve economies of scale, leading to high production costs and uncompetitive pricing compared to imported vehicles. This dynamic limits the growth of domestic supporting industries and perpetuates a reliance on imports. Despite this, the country has cultivated a relatively strong export-oriented components sector, with products like wire harnesses, aluminium parts, and electronic systems shipped to major markets, including Japan, Thailand, and the US. As of 2017, auto parts accounted for 99% of the Philippines' total automotive exports. The DVA share – stable at around 63% – largely reflects labour-intensive production using locally procured inputs. However, some reliance on imported raw materials, particularly from Japan, China, and Korea, persists (Kuroiwa, 2017).

While the Philippines' automotive policy history dates back to the 1970s with programmes focused on local content and market rationalisation, its recent initiative – the Comprehensive Automotive Resurgence Strategy (CARS) – aims to attract foreign automakers and encourage the development of local suppliers. However, technology upgrading has been uneven. Filipino-owned firms often demonstrate greater initiative in forming external linkages and pursuing licensing arrangements, whereas foreign subsidiaries tend to rely heavily on their parent companies. Nevertheless, the small domestic market continues to hinder innovation and the development of technological capabilities, especially among lower-tier suppliers. The limited scope of the country's GVC participation, mainly in component manufacturing, and the absence of large-scale vehicle production remain significant constraints. Although CARS mandates OEMs to localise parts production, its long-term impact remains unclear.

4.3.8 Singapore

Singapore's automotive industry is relatively small in terms of production but strategically positioned within GVCs through its strong industrial and service infrastructure. By leveraging its globally competitive sectors – such as electronics, semiconductors, aviation, and logistics – Singapore has successfully integrated into the regional automotive market, particularly through the distribution of completely built-up cars and the export of auto electronics. Major automotive trade partners include Australia, Indonesia, Malaysia, the Philippines, and Thailand. Despite limited local vehicle assembly, Singapore ranks second only to Thailand in gross automotive export volume among ASEAN countries.

It has also emerged as a leader in autonomous vehicle readiness, ranking first in Asia and second globally in 2018–2019, reflecting its ambition to lead innovation in the regional mobility market (KPMG, 2019).

Singapore's participation in the automotive GVC is characterised by a balanced share of DVA and FVA, with both growing steadily over the years. The FVA reflects imported inputs for high-tech manufacturing and regional redistribution, while the DVA stems from the country's value-adding activities in electronics and logistics. To address challenges such as high wages and deindustrialisation, Singapore has adopted a forward-looking strategy focusing on automation, the formation of dynamic industrial clusters, and the reorganisation of value chains. By integrating its core industries into emerging sectors such as automotive technology, Singapore promotes cross-industry innovation and aims to move upstream in GVCs, capitalising on its skilled workforce and knowledge-based economy.

4.3.9 Thailand

Thailand has emerged as the leading automotive production hub in ASEAN and one of the largest global exporters of vehicles. Nicknamed the 'Detroit of the East', Thailand's automotive industry has evolved over five decades, supported by government policies that promote localisation, FDI, and industrial clustering (Board of Investment (BOI), Thailand, 2017; Dowlah, 2018). In 2017, Thailand ranked 12th globally in automotive production, with exports accounting for 60% of the two million vehicles produced that year (Dowlah, 2018). Its strategic advantages include a skilled but relatively low-cost workforce, efficient logistics infrastructure, and integration into global and regional supply chains. Japanese OEMs dominate the market, holding an 85% share, and have spurred the development of a robust Tier-1 supplier base. However, technological upgrading has primarily been confined to MNCs, while most domestic firms remain in lower tiers with limited capabilities and minimal knowledge transfer. Despite a relatively low DVA share, the country's DVA volume is primarily driven by labour-intensive activities rather than technological advancement.

Government strategies, such as the designation of product champions like one-ton pickup trucks and eco-cars, have successfully attracted new investments and supported the export-oriented growth of the sector. Policy tools – including local content requirements, tax incentives, and the liberalisation of foreign ownership – helped transform Thailand into a base for global green vehicle production. Technological upgrading has gained momentum since the 2000s, as MNCs have established R&D centres focused on product design, testing, and adaptation to the ASEAN market. Nevertheless, only a few domestic suppliers have successfully moved up the value chain. Most Tier-2 and Tier-3 local firms face challenges in scaling innovation and developing capabilities, partly due to weak university-industry linkages and limited spillovers from MNCs. To address these gaps, the government has launched Industry 4.0 policies and established institutions such as the Thailand Automotive Institute to promote innovation, skills development, and collaboration within the sector. Maintaining competitiveness will require reducing dependence on labour-cost advantages and increasing investment in domestic innovation and technological capacity.

4.3.10 Vietnam

Vietnam's automobile industry remains relatively underdeveloped compared to other ASEAN countries, primarily due to its small domestic market and weak supporting industries (Japan International Cooperation Agency (JICA), 2016). Since its inception in 1991, the industry has been dominated by joint ventures with foreign companies, such as Toyota and Honda. In 2018, car sales exceeded production, highlighting the country's reliance on imports, particularly for completely built-up vehicles. Most auto parts and high-value components are still imported, as local production focuses on labour-intensive parts. Domestic assemblers and suppliers struggle to achieve economies of scale with limited technological capacity and low localisation rates. Although the country recorded a nineteen-fold increase in DVA volume between 1990 and 2015, this growth was primarily driven by assembly-line labour rather than technological capability or local sourcing. Consequently, Vietnam remains stuck in a cycle of high production costs, low innovation, and underdeveloped supplier networks.

The Vietnamese government has introduced several policies, including the Automotive Industry Development Plan and Decree 116, to strengthen local manufacturing and increase participation in GVCs. Tariff reductions under ASEAN trade agreements and targeted incentives aim to boost localisation and competitiveness. Nevertheless, the industry's structure – comprising a limited number of assemblers and a relatively small base of domestic parts suppliers – continues to limit its potential. Technological upgrading remains a significant hurdle, with minimal spillovers from MNCs and weak linkages between domestic and foreign firms. While some local companies have shown initiative, most still grapple with basic production technologies. Overcoming these barriers will require stronger policies to foster innovation, scale up supplier networks, and develop core technological competencies.

4.4 Conclusion

ASEAN requires a comprehensive policy framework for the automotive industry to support deeper integration and technological upgrading within GVCs and RVCs. This framework should emphasise the empowerment of domestic firms – particularly SMEs – to enhance their roles within the value chain. Capacity-building efforts should focus on R&D, innovation, and advanced engineering to enable these firms to move up to higher tiers of production.

Given the dominance of SMEs in ASEAN's second and third-tier supplier networks, targeted support is essential to facilitate their GVC entry and upgrading. Local firms lack visibility among global clients, especially in developed economies. Governments should invest in centralised information centres to disseminate customer and market data and actively organise business-matching programmes that connect local, lower-tier suppliers with both foreign and domestic Tier-1 suppliers. While such initiatives exist in some ASEAN countries, they are often fragmented, underfunded, and not explicitly tailored to the automotive sector. A more institutionalised approach, involving collaboration between the public and private sectors, is urgently needed.

A key policy priority is the creation of a joint ASEAN-wide supplier database categorised by firm size and area of specialisation. Such a database would complement existing trade frameworks, such as the AFTA and the RCEP. Additionally, countries should leverage mutual recognition agreements and promote regional certification schemes for automotive-related skills and professional standards. These measures would lay the foundation for cross-border personnel exchange programmes, facilitating the movement of technical experts and knowledge across ASEAN.

Moreover, a regional directory of automotive experts from academia and industry should be developed and regularly updated to support workforce development. This would serve as a resource for cross-national technical exchange and collaborative innovation. SMEs should also be encouraged and supported to join international industry associations and global supplier networks, allowing them to gain exposure to best practices, expand customer bases, and tap into new knowledge ecosystems. Evidence suggests that firms participating in international networking activities, including trade fairs, are more likely to acquire new technologies and engage in innovation.

Current government support schemes – often limited to generic investment incentives – should be complemented by targeted matching grants. These grants could support specific upgrading activities such as product design, branding, prototyping, and advanced engineering. Financial assistance could also extend to recruiting external experts, particularly engineers and technicians from

MNCs, to help SMEs enhance their quality systems and production efficiency. Governments could subsidise a portion of these experts' salaries during the early phases of cooperation to reduce cost barriers.

Finally, collaboration should be encouraged between local firms, universities, and public research institutions. These partnerships should prioritise the development of critical knowledge and skills needed for firms to ascend the value chain. Specific areas of collaboration could include joint research in advanced engineering, product design, and green mobility technologies; technical exchange programmes between universities and automotive firms; and training initiatives to improve productivity and quality. Governments can also support industry-academia linkages by co-funding expert placements – such as engineers or technicians from MNCs – within domestic firms. Public investment in technical education, automotive engineering, and applied research will be vital in preparing ASEAN's workforce for a future of green mobility, electrification, and intelligent transport systems.

5 Conclusions

The integration of ASEAN economies into GVCs has been a defining feature of their recent industrial transformation. Countries such as Malaysia, Thailand, and Vietnam have leveraged GVC participation to accelerate economic growth by aligning with export-oriented manufacturing and engaging with multinational enterprises (MNEs). This Element has explored the opportunities and limitations of GVC participation across three strategically important sectors: agribusiness (coffee), textiles and clothing, and the automotive industry. Drawing from these empirical case studies, this concluding section reflects on the broader implications of GVC participation for ASEAN's development pathways, identifies key structural risks, and outlines policy directions necessary to transform GVC integration into inclusive and sustainable growth.

5.1 GVC Participation and Development

GVCs offer developing economies a viable route to industrialisation by enabling firms to specialise in specific segments of production, such as assembly or processing, without needing to build entire industries from scratch. This approach has been particularly effective for ASEAN countries in generating exports, creating jobs, and attracting foreign direct investment. For example, Vietnam's integration into electronics and Thailand's participation in automobile assembly illustrate how GVCs can support early stage economic upgrading.

However, the benefits of GVC participation are not automatic. The case studies in this Element reveal that many ASEAN countries remain entrenched in lower-value-added segments of global production networks. The share of DVA in exports has grown only marginally, indicating limited progress in moving up the value chain. Firms often rely heavily on imported intermediate goods and foreign-controlled production processes, leading to an overreliance on external technologies and knowledge. This structural condition contributes to what has been referred to as the middle-income trap and the middle-income technology trap, where countries struggle to transition from efficiency-driven to innovation-driven economies.

5.2 Structural Risks and Development Challenges

Across agribusiness (coffee), textiles and clothing, and automobiles, the empirical sections identify a set of interlinked structural challenges that cut across sectors despite differences in technology intensity and market structure. In all three sectors, GVC participation in ASEAN is characterised by passive integration, with local firms and producers concentrated in labour-intensive or low-value functions, such as primary production, assembly, or basic component manufacturing, while high-value activities, including R&D, branding, design, and logistics, remain concentrated among lead firms in advanced economies. As a result, domestic value capture remains limited even in countries with strong export performance. Weak backward and forward linkages further constrain knowledge diffusion and functional upgrading, particularly for SMEs, reinforcing dependence on imported intermediates, foreign-controlled production processes, and external governance structures. A cross-cutting challenge is the limited accumulation of technological capabilities, which exposes ASEAN economies to global supply chain shocks and constrains transitions toward innovation-driven growth.

While these structural risks are shared, they manifest differently across sectors due to variations in GVC governance and production organisation. In buyer-driven chains such as coffee and T&C, asymmetric bargaining power between global buyers and local producers reinforces unequal value capture and weakens incentives for local investment in productivity and innovation. In contrast, the automotive sector follows a producer-driven model coordinated by multinational assemblers and Tier-1 suppliers, in which modular production systems and stringent technical standards limit interactions between lead firms and suppliers, isolating domestic firms from innovation ecosystems despite their greater potential for technological upgrading. Fragmented coordination also differs by sector: in coffee, weak midstream coordination and the presence of intermediary actors constrain inclusive upgrading, while in manufacturing sectors, tiered supplier networks deepen reliance on imported inputs and restrict functional upgrading. Sector-specific social and sustainability risks further differentiate outcomes: rural livelihoods and climate vulnerability in coffee; labour conditions and compliance pressures in textiles and clothing; and skills and technological gaps in automobiles.

These similarities and differences underscore that ASEAN's structural challenges stem not only from sectoral characteristics but from how GVC participation is governed and supported domestically. Across sectors, overreliance on foreign inputs and governance, weak domestic linkages, and limited technological learning constrain innovation-led upgrading and heighten vulnerability to external shocks. Without coordinated policies to strengthen domestic capabilities, improve value chain governance, and foster technological learning, GVC integration – while generating growth and employment – risks locking ASEAN economies into low-value trajectories and limiting the prospects for inclusive and resilient development.

5.3 Navigating the Impacts of Rising US Protectionism

Over recent decades, ASEAN economies have relied heavily on international trade and participation in GVCs as engines of industrialisation, employment creation, and poverty reduction. The resurgence of US protectionism – most notably the enforcement of reciprocal tariff measures in 2025 – poses a significant challenge to this development model. Given ASEAN's deep integration into GVCs and strong dependence on external demand, rising tariff barriers threaten export-led growth, foreign direct investment, and ongoing industrial upgrading.

Several ASEAN member states, including Indonesia, Malaysia, the Philippines, Thailand, and Vietnam, have been directly affected by new US trade measures due to persistent trade surpluses, tariff differentials, and concerns over non-tariff barriers and transhipment risks. These pressures have weakened export competitiveness and increased compliance costs, while heightened scrutiny of production linkages with China has reduced ASEAN's attractiveness as an alternative manufacturing base.

UNIDO and WIFO (2026) indicate that tariff escalation, whether unilateral or retaliatory, generates widespread and asymmetric disruptions to manufacturing value added, labour markets, and poverty outcomes across ASEAN. Any short-term gains from trade diversion are typically modest and temporary, while sustained contractions in manufacturing value drive added longer-term effects, particularly in export-oriented sectors such as electronics, apparel, and motor vehicles. SMEs and women workers are disproportionately affected due to their concentration in labour-intensive and upstream segments of GVCs.

Overall, sustained tariff escalation underscores ASEAN's vulnerability to inward-looking trade policies in major economies and highlights the need for trade diversification, stronger RVCs, and enhanced domestic buffers to support resilient and inclusive industrial development.

5.4 Policy Directions towards Inclusive and Sustainable GVCs

To maximise the benefits of GVC participation and mitigate associated risks, ASEAN countries must adopt a proactive upgrading strategy anchored in innovation, domestic capability-building, digital transformation, and regional collaboration.

First, governments should focus not merely on joining GVCs but on upgrading within them. Policies should support functional, product, and process upgrading through targeted investments in R&D, workforce development, and digital infrastructure. Collaborations between domestic firms and MNEs must be strategically guided to promote knowledge spillovers and value retention. In this context, public research institutes can play a critical intermediary role by supporting firms in identifying, assessing, and adapting imported technologies. Rather than focusing solely on frontier innovation, public research institutes can help screen appropriate foreign technologies, evaluate potential international partners, and facilitate the absorption and adaptation of imported know-how to local production conditions, thereby reducing information asymmetries and the risks associated with costly technology imports (Yoshitomi, 2003). Digitalisation plays a vital role in this transformation. Empirical evidence suggests that basic digital tools can significantly enhance SME formalisation and increase their likelihood of participating in GVCs (Korwatanasakul, 2020, 2023c, 2024). Policies aimed at boosting digital connectivity among informal and small enterprises – through affordable internet access, information technology training, and digital infrastructure – can serve as cost-effective catalysts for both formalisation and deeper GVC engagement.

Second, empowering local SMEs is crucial. Capacity-building programmes, improved access to finance, and stronger support for compliance with international standards can enhance SMEs' competitiveness and integration into higher value segments of GVCs. Public–private partnerships and local supplier development programmes should be scaled up across sectors. Efforts to enhance digital readiness among SMEs – such as introducing digital skills into education curricula, promoting digital literacy, and providing grants to support information and communication technology adoption – will be essential to enabling them to thrive in digitally driven GVC environments.

Third, trade diversification and regional cooperation must become a strategic priority. ASEAN economies should reduce their overreliance on a few major markets by expanding into new geographies and sectors, while simultaneously deepening RVCs through platforms like the RCEP and the ASEAN Economic Community. This will help buffer external shocks and mitigate the effects of rising trade tensions between major powers. ASEAN-wide initiatives to harmonise certification standards, share supplier databases, and promote regional clusters can strengthen RVCs and reduce dependence on extra-regional lead firms. Collective investment in innovation ecosystems and regional knowledge hubs can facilitate the transition from passive to active GVC integration. Upgrading domestic industrial capabilities – particularly among SMEs – remains a linchpin of this strategy.

Fourth, ASEAN must maintain strategic neutrality amid escalating geopolitical rivalries. In light of intensifying US–China competition, the region must balance economic ties with both sides, preserving flexibility and market access while avoiding entanglement in polarised trade alignments. A coordinated, region-wide posture – emphasising autonomy, resilience, and rule-based trade engagement – will be critical to navigating the shifting global trade landscape.

Finally, policy frameworks must promote social upgrading in tandem with economic upgrading. Labour rights, gender equality, and decent work conditions should be embedded in industrial strategies. Environmental sustainability must also be mainstreamed, with incentives for cleaner production, green technologies, and resource efficiency.

5.5 Moving Forward

The ASEAN experience with GVCs illustrates a dual reality. On the one hand, GVC participation has facilitated rapid industrial growth, increased employment, and expanded exports. On the other hand, it has entrenched structural vulnerabilities that limit long-term development and resilience. The empirical insights from the coffee, textile, and automotive sectors in this Element underscore that GVC-led growth is not inherently inclusive or sustainable.

To turn GVCs into engines of equitable development, ASEAN economies must reframe their approach – moving from low-cost participation to strategic upgrading, from foreign dependency to domestic capability, and from fragmented engagement to coordinated regional action. Only through such a shift can GVC participation support the broader goals of innovation-driven, socially just, and environmentally responsible development in the region.

Abbreviations

AFTA	ASEAN Free Trade Area
ASEAN	Association of Southeast Asian Nations
CAGR	compound annual growth rate
CARS	Comprehensive Automotive Resurgence Strategy
CPTPP	Comprehensive and Progressive Agreement for Trans–Pacific Partnership
DVA	domestic value added
DVX	domestic value added in exports used in other countries' exports
EU	European Union
FDI	foreign direct investment
FVA	foreign value added
GDP	gross domestic product
GVC	global value chain
ICO	International Coffee Organization
ILO	International Labour Organization
MNC	multinational corporation
MNE	multinational enterprise
OEC	Observatory of Economic Complexity
OEM	original equipment manufacturer
Lao PDR	Lao People's Democratic Republic
R&D	research and development
RCEP	Regional Comprehensive Economic Partnership
RVC	regional value chain
SME	small and medium-sized enterprise
T&C	textile and clothing
US	United States

References

Alissar, C. (2025). *Retaining Women in Cambodia's Workforce after LDC Graduation*, UNDP.

APEC Study Center. (2017). *Study of SMEs' Integration into Global Value Chains in Services Industries – Fashion Design*, Hong Kong: APEC Study Center, the Chinese University of Hong Kong.

ASEAN. (2021). *Framework for Circular Economy for the ASEAN Economic Community*, Jakarta: ASEAN Secretariat, pp. 1–12.

ASEAN-Japan Centre. (2019). *Paper 1: A Regional Perspective (Global value chains in ASEAN)*, Tokyo: ASEAN-Japan Centre.

ASEAN Main Portal. (2024). *Garment Industry in CLMV Economies*, https://asean.org/wp-content/uploads/2024/12/Textiles-Industry-in-CLMV-Economies.pdf. (Accessed: 20 January 2025).

ASEAN Secretariat. (2023). *ASEAN Statistical Yearbook 2023*, Jakarta: ASEAN Secretariat.

ASEAN Secretariat. (2025). *Trade in Goods (IMTS), Annually, HS 2-digit up to 8-digit (AHTN), in US$*, https://data.aseanstats.org/trade-annually.

Asian Development Bank (2013, August 9). Vietnam labor and employment: Skills training for jobs. Asian Development Bank. Retrieved from https://www.adb.org/features/preparing-viet-nams-workers-today-jobs-tomorrow-report-card (Accessed: 30 May 2026).

Asia-Pacific Economic Cooperation (2025). APEC Workshop on supporting MSMEs' transition to circular economy in textile and garment industries. APEC Small and Medium Enterprises Working Group. APEC Secretariat. Retrieved from https://www.apec.org/docs/default-source/publications/2025/9/225_sme_apec-workshop-on-supporting-msmes-transition-to-circular-economy-in-textile-and-garment-industries.pdf?sfvrsn=c555ddc_1 (Accessed: 30 May 2026).

Azavedo, M. (2024). Arabica coffee bean growing in the Chiang Rai and Chiang Mai areas of Northern Thailand and how to make the farming more sustainable. *British Journal of Environmental Studies*, 4(2), 9–19.

Baldwin, R. E. (2011). *21st Century Regionalism: Filling the gap between 21st century trade and 20th century trade rules*, CEPR Policy Insight.

Bangkok Post. (2025). *Creating a Stir in Instant Coffee*, www.bangkokpost.com/business/general/3006341/creating-a-stir-in-instant-coffee.

Barrientos, S., Gereffi, G., & Rossi, A. (2011). Economic and social upgrading in global production networks: A new paradigm for a changing world. *International Labour Review*, 150(3–4), 319–340.

BASIC. (2018). *Coffee: The hidden crisis behind the success.* Commerce Équitable France & Max Havelaar France, https://basic.coop/en/productions/etude/coffee-the-success-story-hiding-a-crisis/.

BASIC. (2024). *The grounds for sharing: A study of value distribution in the coffee industry.* Solidaridad Network. www.solidaridadnetwork.org/publications/the-grounds-for-sharing-a-study-of-value-distribution-in-the-coffee-industry/.

Bellemare, M. F., Bloem, J. R., & Lim, S. (2022). Producers, consumers, and value chains in low- and middle-income countries. In C. B. Barrett & D. R. Just, eds., *Handbook of Agricultural Economics*. North Holland: Elsevier, 4933–4996.

Berger, A., Bruhn, D., Bender, A., et al. (2016). *Deep Preferential Trade Agreements and Upgrading in Global Value Chains: The Case of Vietnam*, Bonn: The German Development Institute.

Bernhardt, T. (2013). Developing Countries in the Global Apparel Value Chain: A Tale of Upgrading and Downgrading Experiences. Working Paper No. 22, *Capturing the Gains: Economic and Social Upgrading in Global Production Networks and Trade*. Manchester, http://dx.doi.org/10.2139/ssrn.2237490.

Board of Investment (Thailand). (2017). *Thailand's Automotive Industry: the Next-Generation*. Bangkok.

Bühler Group. (2025). The Bühler Group: Locations, www.buhlergroup.com/global/en/locations.html.

Bui, K. (2025). Textile rules of origin in CPTPP: More flexible provisions, *Vietnam Economic News*, 8 September.

Cahyoputra, L. A. L. (2024). *Textile Industry Crisis: Factory Closures and Nearly 14,000 Layoffs Due to Imported Goods*. JakataGlobe.ID. https://jakartaglobe.id/business/textile-industry-crisis-factory-closures-and-nearly-14000-layoffs-due-to-imported-goods?utm_source=chatgpt.com#goog_rewarded.

Center for WTO and International Trade – VCCI. (2024). *Opening opportunities for Vietnam's textile and garment industry to the EU Market*. https://wtocenter.vn/tin-tuc/25831-opening-opportunities-for-vietnams-textile-and-garment-industry-to-the-eu-market (accessed 26 December 2025).

Chang, J. H., Rynhart, G., & Huynh, P. (2016). *ASEAN in Transformation. Textiles, Clothing and Footwear: Refashioning the Future*. Bureau for Employers' Activities (ACT/EMP), Working Paper.

Cucagnaa, M. E. & Goldsmith, P. D. (2018). Value adding in the agri-food value chain. *International Food and Agribusiness Management Review*, 21(3), 294–316.

Daly, J., Hamrick, D., Bamber, P., & Fernandez-Stark, K. (2018). *Jamaica in the Arabica Coffee Global Value Chain*. Durham: Duke University Global Value Chains Center.

Dang, C. L., Trinh, T. N., Vu, H. T. T., & Diep Thi Bich Le. (2024). *Vietnam | Fashion Law Guide 2024*, Tilleke and Gibbins.

Devaux, A., Torero, M., Donovan, J., & Horton, D. (2018). Agricultural innovation and inclusive value-chain development: A Review. *Journal of Agribusiness in Developing and Emerging Economies*, 8(1), 99–123.

DiCaprio, A. & Suvannaphakdy, S. (2017). *Are Least Developed Countries Sidelined in Advanced Manufacturing Production Networks?* ADBI Working Paper 711. Tokyo: Asian Development Bank Institute.

Doi Chaang Coffee. (2025). *Craft & Selected Lots (Grand Cru Quality Series)*, https://doichaangcoffee.co.th/en/craft-selected-lots/.

Dollar, D. & Kidder, M. (2017). *Institutional quality and participation in global value chains, Global Value Chain Report*, WTO, pp. 161–173.

Dowlah C. (2018). Global Value Chains in Automobiles. In C. Dowlah, ed, *Transformations of Global Prosperity*. Cham: Palgrave Macmillan, 199–230.

Embassy of Brazil in Bangkok. (2021). *Market Research in Thailand: Coffee, Premium and Standard, Green and Roasted Beans*. Bangkok: Embassy of Brazil in Bangkok.

ERIA/OECD. (2024), *SME Policy Index: ASEAN 2024 – Enabling Sustainable Growth and Digitalisation*, Jakarta: ERIA/Paris: OECD.

EU International Partnerships. (2019). *SMART Myanmar II*, https://international-partnerships.ec.europa.eu/policies/programming/projects/smart-myanmar-ii_en (Accessed 20 February 2025).

Eurocham Myanmar. (2023). *Myanmar Garment Sector Factsheet Version 2.0.* https://eurocham-myanmar.org/wp-content/uploads/2023/11/Myanmar-Garment-Sector-Factsheet_November-2023.pdf (Accessed: 20 January 2025).

Euromonitor International. (2024). *What's Next for Coffee Shops in Southeast Asia*, www.euromonitor.com/article/whats-next-for-coffee-shops-in-southeast-asia.

European Commission (EU). (2022). *EU Strategy for Sustainable and Circular Textiles. European Commission*. Brussels: European Commission.

Eversys. (2025). *Eversys Legacy*, https://legacy.eversys.com.

Fernandez-Stark, K., Bamber, P., & Gereffi, G. (2012). *Inclusion of Small- and Medium-Sized Producers in High-Value Agro-Food Value Chain*. Durham: Duke University Center on Globalization, Governance & Competitiveness.

Frederik, S. (2024). *Sustainable Industrial Policies and Strategies in the Textiles and Clothing Sector-Lessons Learned from Cambodia, Jordan and Vietnam*, No. 130. International Labour Organization.

Gabriel, P. Y. & Lubis, M. M. (2025). Sustainability analysis of coffee agribusiness in Indonesia. *International Journal of Health, Economics, and Social Sciences*, 7(2), 788–795.

Gama, A., Saget, C., & Elsheikhi, A. (2018). *Labour Market Inventory ASEAN 201015: Labour Market Policy in an Age of Increasing Economic Integration*. Geneva: International Labour Organization.

GDPS-MOE. (2022). *Cambodia's Roadmap for Sustainable Consumption and Production 2022–2035*. Phnom Penh: Ministry of Environment.

General Department of Customs and Excise of Cambodia. (2026). *International Merchandise Trade Statistics: Data Search by HS Code*, https://stats.customs.gov.kh/en/data-search/by-hs-code.

Gereffi, G. (1999). International trade and industrial upgrading in the apparel commodity chain. *Journal of International Economics*, 48(1), 37–70.

Gereffi, G., Humphrey, J., & Sturgeon, T. (2005). The governance of global value chains. *Review of International Political Economy*, 12(1), 78–104.

Global Fashion Agenda (GFA). (2024). *Establishing a Vision & Roadmap for Circular Fashion in Vietnam*.

Global Standard. (2026). *Global Organic Textile Standard Annual Report 2025: Ecology & Social Responsibility*. Stuttgart: Global Standard.

Goto, K. (2007). Industrial upgrading of the Vietnamese garment industry: An analysis from the global value chains perspective. *RCAPS Working Paper*, 7, 1–16.

Goto, K. (2011). Competitiveness and decent work in global value chains: Substitutionary or complementary? *Development in Practice*, 21(7), 943–958.

Goto, K. (2023). Viet Nam's Textile and Garment Industry in the Global Value Chain.

Grabs, J. (2017). The rise of buyer-driven sustainability governance: Emerging trends in the global coffee sector. *ZenTra Working Paper in Transnational Studies*, No. 73/2017.

Grabs, J. & Ponte, S. (2019). The evolution of power in the global coffee value chain and production network. *Journal of Economic Geography*, 19(4), 803–828.

Ha, L., Hoa, N. X., Yen, D., Thao, L., & Giam, D. (2025). A review of research and technology transfer in agricultural universities: Practical issues in Vietnam. *Vietnam Journal of Agricultural Sciences*, 8(1), 2426–2441.

Hatsukano, N. & Tanaka, K. (2014). Challenges to make Cambodian SMEs participate in global value chains: Towards addressing poverty and inequality. In N. Hatsukano & I. Kuroiwa, eds., *Inclusive Development in the Era of Economic Integration: Policy Implications for LDCs*. Bangkok: Bangkok Research Center, IDE-JETRO.

Hill, E., Baird, M., & Seetahul, S. (2020). The Philippines and COVID-19: Impact on the Private Sector. The Australian Women's Working Futures Project. The Women and Work Research Group. https://asiapacific.unwomen.org/en/digital-library/publications/2020/08/the-philippines-and-covid-19-impact-on-the-private-sector.

Hirpato, A. D. (2022). Value chain analysis of coffee product in the case of Sidama Region, Ethiopia. *Journal of Research in Business and Management*, 10(4), 1–15.

Hoan, P. T. & Hung, P. X. (2024). Determinants of Vietnam's textile exports: An analysis by gravity model. *Journal of Economic Cooperation and Development*, 2(45), 41–64.

Hue, T. T. & Korwatanasakul, U. (2023). Global value chain participation and labour productivity in manufacturing firms in Viet Nam: Firm-level panel analysis. *Institutions and Economies*, 15(4), 35–62.

Humphrey, J., & Schmitz, H. (2002). How does insertion in global value chains affect upgrading in industrial clusters? Regional Studies, 36(9), 1017–1027. https://doi.org/10.1080/0034340022000022198.

ICO. (2024). *Coffee Development Report 2022–23: Beyond Coffee: Towards a Circular Economy in Coffee*. London: ICO.

ICO. (2025). *Coffee Market Report: February 2025*. London: ICO.

ILO Liaison Office in Myanmar. (2015). *Myanmar Garment Sub-Sector Value Chain Analysis*. Yangon: International Labour Organization.

ILO. (2024). *Cambodia Annual Report: An Industry and Compliance Overview for 2022–2023-Better Factories Cambodia*. Geneva.

Intarakumnerd, P. (2011). *How to Enhance Innovation Capability with Internal and External Sources*, ERIA Research Project Report 2010. Jakarta: ERIA.

Intarakumnerd, P. & Korwatanasakul, U. (2020). Business impacts and government supports for firms' upgrading and innovation under COVID-19 in Southeast Asia. *STEPI S&T Policy Journal (과학기술정책)*, 3(2), 33–65.

International Labour Organization (ILO). (2018). *Improving Labour Relations for Decent Work and Sustainable Development in the Myanmar Garment Industry (ILO-GIP)*. Yangon: ILO Liaison Office in Myanmar.

International Labour Organization (ILO). (2022). *Employment in Myanmar in 2021: A Rapid Assessment*. Bangkok: ILO Regional Office for Asia and the Pacific.

International Labour Organization (ILO). (2025). *Empowering Women in Vietnam's Textile and Garment Industry: The Importance of Training, Skills Development, and Gender Inequality*, https://tinyurl.com/43m559md

ITC. (2021). *Lao PDR: Coffee Sector Export Roadmap (2021–2025)*. Geneva: The International Trade Centre (ITC).

ITC. (2021). *The Coffee Guide (4th Edition)*, Geneva: ITC.

Japan External Trade Organization (JETRO). (2018). *The Activity of Myanmar-Japan Joint Initiative*. Yangon: JETRO.

Japan International Cooperation Agency (JICA). (2016). *A Research on Supporting Industry for Automobile Assemblers in Vietnam*. Ha Noi: JICA.

JDE Peet. (2025). *JDE Peet's 2024 Annual Report*, Amsterdam: JDE Peet.

Kaiser, U. (2018). *Indonesia AutoBook 2018*. Radolfzell: Kaiser International Limited.

Kaplinsky, R. & Morris, M. (2002). *A Handbook for Value Chain Research*. September, pp. 4–7, Brighton: Institute for Development Studies.

Keawsuwan, P. (2015). *The Challenges of Auto Parts Industry in ASEAN*, Presentation material at Auto Parts Tech Day, 27 May. Bangkok. www.sciencepark.or.th/documents/downloads/Challenges%20of%20Auto%20Parts%20Industry%20in%20ASEAN.pdf.

Korwatanasakul, U. (2019). *Paper 10: Thailand (Global value chains in ASEAN)*, Tokyo: ASEAN-Japan Centre.

Korwatanasakul, U. (2020). Global value chains, digitalisation, and digital readiness: A firm-level analysis with a focus on Asian small and medium-sized enterprises. In KAS SOPAS, ed., *Digitalisation, Trade, and Geopolitics in Asia*, Tokyo: KAS SOPAS, pp. 21–48.

Korwatanasakul, U. (2023a). Thailand and the middle-income trap: An analysis from the global value chain perspective. *Institutions and Economies*, 15(4), 7–33.

Korwatanasakul, U. (2023b). Global value chains and Vietnam's economic development: A path to perils or prosperity? In T. Vu & N. Truong, eds., *The Dragon's Underbelly: Dynamics and Dilemmas in Vietnam's Economy and Politics*. Singapore: ISEAS Publishing, pp.73–107.

Korwatanasakul, U. (2023c). The role of digitalization in firms' global value chain participation in Asia and the Pacific. In S. Bera, Y. Yao, A. Palit, & D. B. Rahut, eds., *Digital Transformation for Inclusive and Sustainable Development in Asia*. Tokyo: ADBI, pp. 188–210.

Korwatanasakul, U. (2024). Unlocking inclusive growth: The nexus of digitalization, formalization, and global value chains. In D. Azhgaliyeva, K. Jungwook, & S. Tian, eds., *Beyond Boundaries: Navigating the Digital Landscape for a Green and Inclusive Future*. Tokyo: ADBI, pp. 145–168.

Korwatanasakul, U. (2026). The dynamics of overlapping agreements: Sequencing, layering, and feedback in East Asian regionalism. *European Journal of East Asian Studies*, https://doi.org/10.1163/15700615-tat00003

Korwatanasakul, U., Baek, Y., & Majoe, A. (2022). Analysis of global value chain participation and workers' wages in Thailand: A micro-level analysis. *The Singapore Economic Review*, https://doi.org/10.1142/S021759082250045X.

Korwatanasakul, U. & Intarakumnerd, P. (2020). *Paper 12: Automobiles (Global value chains in ASEAN)*, Tokyo: ASEAN-Japan Centre.

Korwatanasakul, U. & Intarakumnerd, P. (2021). *Paper 13: Electronics (Global value chains in ASEAN)*, Tokyo: ASEAN-Japan Centre.

Korwatanasakul, U. & Paweenawat, S.W. (2021). Trade, global value chains, and small and medium-sized enterprises in Thailand: A firm-level panel analysis. In S. Urata, ed., *Enhancing SME Participation in Global Value Chains: Determinants, Challenges, and Policy Recommendations*. Tokyo, ADBI, pp. 166–191.

Korwatanasakul, U. & Purbantina, A.P. (2021). *Paper 4: Indonesia (Global value chains in ASEAN)*, Tokyo: ASEAN-Japan Centre.

Korwatanasakul, U. & Purbantina, A. P. (2022). Sub-Pillar F – Enhancing participation in Global Value Chains. In *'SEAN Integration Report 2022, Kuala Lumpur: IDEAS*, pp. 111–129.

KPMG. (2019). *Autonomous Vehicles Readiness Index*. Zurich: KPMG International.

Kraft Heinz. (2021). Ethical Bean: From Crop to Cup, www.kraftheinzcompany.com/esg/story-ethical-bean.html.

Kresnawati. (2024). [Interview] (6 August).

Kudo, T. (2012). How has the Myanmar garment industry evolved? In T. Fukunishi, ed., *Dynamics of the Garment Industry in Low-Income Countries: Experience of Asia and Africa*. Chiba: Institute of Developing Economies, pp. 67–97.

Kuroiwa, I. (2017). *The Structure of the Automobile Value Chain in Southeast Asia*, BRC Research Report No. 16, Bangkok: JETRO.

La Marzocco (2025). *Our History*, www.lamarzocco.com/ae/en/about-us/history/.

Lacazza World. (2022). *Blend for Better*, www.lavazza.com/en/blend-for-better.

Lalu, B., Deb, A., & Suman, S. (2025). Institutional engagement and its role in livelihood transformation of tribal coffee farmers in Araku Valley. *Indian Journal of Extension Education*, 61(3), 308–322.

Law on Investment of the Kingdom of Cambodia. (2021). *Royal Kram No. 1021/014, promulgated 15 October 2021.* Phnom Penh: Royal Government of Cambodia.

Le, D. D. (2015). The past and the hopeful future of Vietnam's economy. *Asian Management Insights*, 2(1), 28–35.

Lee, J. W. & Wie, D. (2015). Technological change, skill demand, and wage inequality: Evidence from Indonesia. *World Development*, 67, 238–250.

Lee, K., Qu, D., & Mao, Z. (2021). Global value chains, industrial policy, and industrial upgrading: Automotive sectors in Malaysia, Thailand, and China in comparison with Korea. *European Journal of Development Research*, 33(2), 275–303.

Leogap. (2025). *Our Brand*, www.leogap.com/en/company/about-us/our-brand/.

MGTC. (2024). *Green Investment Tax Allowance (GITA) Asset 2024.* Selangor Darul Ehsan: Malaysian Green Technology and Climate Change Corporation (MGTC).

Marklines, Macroeconomic statistics from Fitch, PwC Research and Analysis ASEAN-6 Automotive Market Snapshot. www.pwc.com/vn/en/publications/2025/asean-automative-market.pdf.

Maspul, K. A. (2024). Exploring tourism and economic growth in Bangkok's specialty coffee. *Jurnal Ekonomi LLDikti Wilayah 1*, 3(1), 1–8.

Ministry of International Trade and Industry (Malaysia). (2017). *Automotive Industry.* www.miti.gov.my/index.php/pages/view/374.

Momentum Works. (2023). *Coffee in Southeast Asia: Modernising retail of the daily beverage*, Singapore: Momentum Works.

Mulyati, H. & Indrawan, D. (2021). Inclusive business models in coffee value chain: Comparing practical evidence between East Java and North Sumatra. *Jurnal Manajemen & Agribisnis*, 18(2), 122–130.

Myanmar Investment Commission. (2020). *FDI worth US$ 1.92 billion injected into Thilawa SEZ.*

Natsuda, K., Goto, K., & Thoburn, J. (2010). Challenges to the Cambodian garment industry in the global garment value chain, *European Journal of Development Research*, 22(4), 469–493.

Natsuda, K. & Thoburn, J. (2018). Industrial policy and the development of the automotive industry in the Philippines. *Canadian Journal of Development Studies/Revue Canadienne d'études du développement*, 39(3), 371–391.

Nelles, W. (2023). Academic network-building for agroecology and sustainable agri-food systems in Southeast Asia: critical reflections on a regional initiative, *Agroecology and Sustainable Food Systems*, 47(1), 126–155.

Nestlé. (2023). *Nestlé Supply Chain Disclosure: Coffee*, www.nestle.com/sites/default/files/2019-07/nestle-supply-chain-disclosure-coffee-tier-1.pdf.

Nestlé Thailand. (2025). *Nestlé is Committed to Investing in Nescafé Production in Thailand*, www.nestle.co.th/en/media/pressreleases/nescafe-news.

Newbery Street Coffee Roasters. (2025). *A Journey Through Thai Coffee: Exploring Farms, Traditions, and the Future of Specialty Coffee*, https://newberyst.com/blogs/coffee/a-journey-through-thai-coffee-exploring-farms-traditions-and-the-future-of-specialty-coffee?srsltid=AfmBOooSs8pe9Gx0I04HDZ8RcSpfEf1bZpvUx_fAFvO9F2dmjEjWMR41.

Nguyen, T. (2016). *Opportunities and Challenges for Vietnam's Textile and Garment Exports in TPP and EU-Vietnam FTA*. International Economics Strategic Analysis for Growth & Development.

Nordic Development Fund. (2016). *Organic Farming Initiatives introduced in Myanmar*. [online] www.ndf.int/newsroom/organic-farming-initiatives-introduced-in-myanmar.html (Accessed 20 February 2025).

OEC. (2025a). *Unroasted Coffee, Not Decaffeinated*, https://oec.world/en/profile/hs/unroasted-coffee-non-decaffeinated.

OEC. (2025b). *Coffee, Whether or Not Roasted or Decaffeinated; Husks and Skins; Coffee Substitutes Containing Coffee in Any Proportion*, https://oec.world/en/profile/hs/coffee.

OEC. (2025c). *Coffee in Thailand*, https://oec.world/en/profile/bilateral-product/coffee/reporter/tha.

OEC. (2025d). *Coffee in Indonesia*, https://oec.world/en/profile/bilateral-product/coffee/reporter/idn.

OEC. (2025e). *Coffee in Vietnam*, https://oec.world/en/profile/bilateral-product/coffee/reporter/vnm.

OEC. (2025f). *Coffee in Laos*, https://oec.world/en/profile/bilateral-product/coffee/reporter/lao.

OECD. (2008). *Enhancing the Role of SMEs in Global Value Chains*. Paris: OECD.

OECD. (2012). *Mapping Global Value Chains*. Paris: OECD.

OECD. (2015). *Participation of Developing Countries in Global Value Chains: Implications for Trade and Trade-Related Policies. OECD Trade Policy Papers*. Paris: OECD.

OECD. (2018). *OECD Due Diligence Guidance for Responsible Supply Chains in the Garment and Footwear Sector*. Paris: OECD Publishing.

OECD. (2021a). *Towards a Skills Strategy for Southeast Asia: Skills for Post-COVID Recovery and Growth*, Paris: OECD.

OECD. (2021b). *Facilitating the Green Transition for ASEAN SMEs, Facilitating the Green Transition for ASEAN SMEs*, Paris: OECD.

OECD. (2023a). *Agricultural Policy Monitoring and Evaluation 2023: Indonesia – Country Chapter*. Paris: OECD.

OECD. (2023b). *OECD Skills Strategy Southeast Asia: Skills for a Post-COVID Recovery and Growth, OECD*, Paris: OECD.

OECD. (2025a). *Agricultural Policy Monitoring and Evaluation 2025*. Paris: OECD.

OECD. (2025b). *Trade in Value Added (TiVA) 2023 Edition*. Paris: OECD.

Onyas, W. I., McEachern, M.G., & Ryan, A. (2018). Co-constructing sustainability: Agencing sustainable coffee farmers in Uganda, *Journal of Rural Studies*, 61, 12–21.

Petroncini. (2019). *IMA Petroncini Roasters and Complete Coffee Processing Plants from A to Z*, https://ima.it/coffee/ima-coffee-petroncini/.

Phimmavong, S., Keenan, R. J., Phimmavong, V., Maroulis, J., & Maraseni, T. (2023). Assessing the COVID-19 impacts on the coffee industry in Laos: An input-output modelling approach. *Cogent Economics & Finance*, 11(2), 1–18.

Pisei, H. (2024). Surge seen in textile exports, *The Phnom Penh Post*, 12 March 2025.

Prime Minister of Vietnam. (2022). Decision No. 1643/QD-TTg Approving the Strategy for Development of Vietnam's Textiles and Clothing, Leather and Footwear Industries to 2030, with a Vision to 2035. Government Portal of the Socialist Republic of Vietnam, https://datafiles.chinhphu.vn/cpp/files/vbpq/2022/12/1643ttg.signed.pdf.

Probat. (2025). *History*, www.probat.com/en/company/about-us/history/.

PWC. (2025). *Green Finance in Vietnam: Pathway to Sustainable Economic Development*.

Qiang, C.Z., Liu, Y., & Steenbergen, V. (2021), *An Investment Perspective on Global Value Chains, An Investment Perspective on Global Value Chains*, Washington: World Bank.

Rancilio Group. (2024). *Who We Are*, www.ranciliogroup.com/who-we-are/.

Rastogi, V. (2018). Cambodia's Garment Manufacturing Industry, *ASEAN Briefing*, 1 November 2025.

Ravindran, S. (2024). 90% of garment units are Chinese-owned, *Khmer Times*.

Raychaudhuri, M. (2025). *ASEAN countries face their own 'China shock'*. www.reuters.com/markets/asia/asean-countries-face-their-own-china-shock-raychaudhuri-2025-05-15/?utm_source=chatgpt.com.

Rifin, A. & Nauly, D. (2020). The impact of involvement in the global value chain on coffee farmers in Indonesia: Case study of Margamulya coffee producer cooperative and Mitra Malabar Cooperative, Bandung, Indonesia. *ADBI Working Paper Series*, no. 1143. Tokyo: Asian Development Bank Institute.

Roy, D. (2017). Agricultural trade. In K. A. Reinert, ed, *Handbook of Globalisation and Development*. Cheltenham: Edward Elgar, pp.59–82.

Royal Government of Cambodia. (2015). *Cambodia Industrial Development Policy 2015 – 2025*. https://cdc.gov.kh/wp-content/uploads/2022/04/IDP-English.pdf (Accessed 21 January 2025).

Sachs, J. D., Cordes, K. Y., Rising, J., Toledano, P., & Maennling, N. (2019). *Ensuring Economic Viability and Sustainability of Coffee Production*. New York: Columbia Center on Sustainable Investment.

Sachs, J., Fornabaio, L., Baraga, B., Massa, I., & Toure, S. (2025). *Prosperity for Coffee Producers through SDG based Coffee Plans*. New York: Columbia Center on Sustainable Investment.

Scolari Engineering. (2025). *Integrated Manufacturing System for Coffee*, www.scolarieng.com.

Simonelli Group. (2025). *History*, https://simonelligroup.com/en/history/.

Sinaga. (2022). [Interview] (21 July 2022).

Sovirak, S. & Kim, K. (2006), *Sustaining Garment Export: A Cambodian Case Study*, No. 12. Cambodian Institute for Cooperation and Peace.

Starbucks. (2025). *Where Does Coffee Come From*, https://athome.starbucks .com/story/where-does-coffee-come.

Starbucks Indonesia. (2025). *Tentang Starbucks Indonesia*, www.starbucks.co .id/starbucks-indonesia-in-the-news.

Statistics Indonesia. (2025). *Estates Production by Month*, www.bps.go.id/ indicator/54/761/10/estates-production-by-month.html.

Sturgeon, T., Daly, J., Frederick, S., Bamber, P., & Gereffi, G. (2016). *The Philippines in the Automotive Global Value Chain*. Center on Globalization, Governance & Competitiveness, Duke University.

Sudiono. (2022). [Interview] (20 July).

Suryana, A. T., Harianto, H., Syaukat, Y., & Harmini, H. (2023). Indonesia robusta coffee value chain: Mapping and upgrading opportunities. *BIO Web of Conferences*, EDP Sciences.

Tampubolon, J., Ginting, A., Nainggolan, H. L., & Tarigan, J. R. (2023). Indonesian coffee development path: Production and international trade. *Asian Journal of Agricultural Extension, Economics & Sociology*, 41(12), 316–328.

Thăng, N. T. H. (2022). The role of Vietnam in the global coffee value chain. *European Journal of Business and Management Research*, 7(3), 48–51.

Thanh, V. T. & Ha, P. H. (2004). Vietnam's Recent Economic Reforms and Developments: Achievements, Paradoxes, and Challenges. In P. Taylor, ed., *Social Inequality in Vietnam and the Challenges to Reform*. Singapore: ISEAS – Yusof Ishak Institute, pp. 63–89.

Thermoplan AG. (2025). *Thermoplan AG*, www.thermoplan.ch/en/home.

Tongurai, J. & Fujioka, T. (2017). Thailand-Plus-One strategy: Practices of Japanese firms in the Greater Mekong Subregion. *FIIB Business Review*, 6(4), 3–9.

Tian, K., Dietzenbacher, E., & Jong-A-Pin, R. (2022). Global value chain participation and its impact on industrial upgrading, *World Economy*, 45(5), 1362–1385.

TradeInt. (2024). *Vietnam Coffee Exports 2023: Most Promising Market?* https://tradeint.com/insights/blogs/vietnam-coffee-exports-2023/.

Trần, A. N. (2012). Vietnamese textile and garment industry in the global supply chain: State strategies and workers' responses, *Institutions and Economies*, 4(3), pp. 123–150.

Tri, V. N. (2000). *Vietnam's Economic Policy since 1975*, Singapore: Institute of Southeast Asian Studies (ISEAS)–Yusof Ishak Institute.

Truong, C. B. (2008). Factors of Agglomeration in Vietnam and Recommendations. In M. Ariff, ed., *Analyses of Industrial Agglomeration, Production Networks and FDI Promotion*. Jakarta: Economic Research Institute for ASEAN and East Asia, pp. 155–89.

Tsuboi, Y. (2007). *Twenty Years after the Adoption of the Doi Moi Policy*. Tokyo: Graduate School of Political Science, Waseda University.

Tumangger & Mulyadi. (2022). [Interview] (19 July).

UNCTAD. (2013). *World Investment Report 2013: Global Value Chains: Investment and Trade for Development*. Geneva: United Nations.

UNIDO. (2024). *Food, Beverages and Tobacco (% of Value Added in Manufacturing)*, https://data.worldbank.org/indicator/NV.MNF.FBTO.ZS.UN.

UNIDO and WIFO. (2026). *The Global Domino Effect: How Rising Tariff Barriers Affect Industries in Developing Economies and Least Developed Countries*. Vienna: United Nations Industrial Development Organization.

USDA. (2024a). *Indonesia: Coffee Semi-Annual (Attaché Report)*. Jakarta: USDA (Office of Agricultural Affairs, Jakarta).

USDA. (2024b). *Vietnam: Coffee Semi-Annual (Attaché Report)*. Hanoi: USDA (Office of Agricultural Affairs, Hanoi).

Utrilla-Catalan, R., Rodríguez-Rivero, R., Narvaez, V. et al. (2022). Growing inequality in the coffee global value chain: A complex network assessment. *Sustainability*, 14(2), 672.

Vicol, M., Neilson, J., Hartatri, D. F. S., & Cooper, P. (2018). Upgrading for whom? Relationship coffee, value chain interventions and rural development in Indonesia. *World Development*, 110(C), 26–37.

Vietnam Investment Review. (2025). *Trung Nguyen Legend Breaks Ground on Southeast Asia's Largest Coffee Factory in Buon Ma Thuot*, https://vir.com.vn/trung-nguyen-legend-breaks-ground-on-southeast-asias-largest-coffee-factory-in-buon-ma-thuot-124215.html.

Vietnam News. (2024). Garment industry improves productivity to reduce pressure from high labour costs. *Vietnam News*, 28 August 2025.

Vietnam Plus. (2024). Vietnam's garment-textile exports expected to reach 44 billion USD this year. *Vietnam Plus*, 15 December 2025.

Vietnam Textile and Apparel Association. (2023). *Vietnam textile and garment industry development strategy to 2030, vision to 2035*. 30 March 2025.

Voice of Vietnam. (2024). Vietnam outpaces Bangladesh to become world's second apparel – textile exporter. *Voice of Vietnam*, December.

Winkler, D. (2022). *Leveraging Foreign Investment for Decent and Productive Jobs*. Geneva: International Labour Organization.

Wongpit, P., Syphoxay, P., Sisoumang, B., & Sykhanthong, S. (2023). Mapping the coffee value chain in Lao PDR: Issues, insights, and strategies. *Research on World Agricultural Economy*, 4(4), 1–9.

World Bank. (2021). *Digital Skills in a Digitizing Vietnam-Assessing the Demand for Digital Skills in Vietnam*. Washington, DC: The World Bank.

World Bank. (2022). *Educate to Grow*. Washington, DC: The World Bank.

World Bank. (2023a). *Challenges amid Conflict: Myanmar Economic Monitor, December 2023*. Washington, DC: World Bank.

World Bank. (2023b). *Myanmar's Garment Industry in 2023*. Washington, DC: The World Bank.

World Bank. (2025a). *Agriculture, Forestry, and Fishing, Value Added (% of GDP)*, https://data.worldbank.org/indicator/NV.AGR.TOTL.ZS.

World Bank. (2025b). *Employment in Agriculture (% of Total Employment) (Modelled ILO Estimate)*, https://data.worldbank.org/indicator/SL.AGR.EMPL.ZS.

World Bank. (2025c). *Food, Beverages and Tobacco (% of Value Added in Manufacturing)*, https://data.worldbank.org/indicator/NV.MNF.FBTO.ZS.UN?CID=AGR_TT_agriculture_EN_EXT&locations=ZJ.

World Bank. (2026a). *Cambodia Textile and Clothing Exports by Country and Region 2020*. World Integrated Trade Solution (WITS), https://tinyurl.com/yc2mbjxb.

World Bank. (2026b). *Myanmar Product Exports and Imports 2023*. World Integrated Trade Solution (WITS), https://tinyurl.com/4b53ry6a.

World Bank. (2026c). *Vietnam Textiles and Clothing Exports by Country and Region 2023*. World Integrated Trade Solution (WITS), https://tinyurl.com/yc5ef95m.

Wright, D. R., Bekessy, S. A., Lentini, P. E. et al. (2024). Sustainable coffee: A review of the diverse initiatives and governance dimensions of global coffee supply chains, *Ambio*, 53(7), 984–1001.

WWF. (2018), *Mapping Existing Policies, Initiatives, Stakeholders and Gaps to Support Textile Sector with Sustainability Transition in Vietnam*. Hanoi: WWF.

Yamaguchi, A. (2018). Global value chains in ASEAN. *Institute for International Monetary Affairs*, 1(1), 1–15.

Yi, J., Meemken, E. M., & Mazariegos-Anastassiou, V. (2021). Post-farmgate food value chains make up most of consumer food expenditures globally. *Nature Food*, 2(6), 417–425.

Yoshitomi, M. (2003). *Post-Crisis Development Paradigms in Asia*. Tokyo: Asian Development Bank Institute.

Yunas, S., Setiarini, & Hermawati, A. (2024). New update of comparative advantage and export growth of ASEAN countries: The case of ASEAN textile industry. *International Journal of Economics, Commerce and Management*, 12(1), 190–209. https://ijecm.co.uk/wp-content/uploads/2024/01/12111.pdf.

Zana, T. & Abayneh, H. (2019). Value chain analysis of coffee product in the case of Sidama Region, Ethiopia. *International Journal of Current Research*, 11(2), 1185–1191.

Executive Summary

This Element examines the dynamics of global value chain (GVC) participation in Southeast Asia, highlighting both its transformative potential and the structural risks it poses for long-term development. Through comparative case studies of agribusiness (coffee), textiles and clothing (T&C), and automobiles, the analysis explores how Association of Southeast Asian Nations (ASEAN) economies engage with GVCs, why deep integration has not always translated into higher domestic value added (DVA), and what policy approaches are needed to ensure that GVC participation supports inclusive and sustainable growth.

Guided by four overarching research questions, the Element asks: (1) how ASEAN economies are positioned within global and regional value chains (RVCs) and what structural factors shape their roles across industries; (2) why deep GVC participation often fails to generate higher DVA and inclusive development outcomes; (3) what constraints limit upgrading and value capture by local firms and small and medium-sized enterprises (SMEs) across countries and sectors; and (4) which policy and institutional frameworks are most effective in leveraging GVC and RVC participation to promote resilient, inclusive, and sustainable sectoral development in ASEAN.

Over recent decades, ASEAN economies – particularly Indonesia, Malaysia, Thailand, and Vietnam – have embraced GVCs as a pathway to rapid industrialisation, export expansion, and job creation. By specialising in specific segments of production, such as assembly or processing, countries have attracted foreign direct investment, gained access to global technologies, and benefited from productivity spillovers through learning-by-exporting and engagement with multinational enterprises (MNEs). In several cases, GVC participation has also supported employment generation and, where forward linkages are stronger, contributed to wage growth and social inclusion.

However, the Element shows that the developmental benefits of GVC participation are neither automatic nor evenly distributed. Across all three sectors, many ASEAN economies remain concentrated in low-value-added activities, including primary agricultural production, garment assembly, and basic component manufacturing. Domestic value added in exports has increased only marginally, reflecting persistent dependence on imported intermediates, foreign-controlled production processes, and external governance structures. These conditions contribute to middle-income and middle-innovation traps, limiting transitions toward innovation-driven growth.

A central finding is the prevalence of passive GVC integration across sectors. High-value activities – such as R&D, branding, design, and logistics – remain concentrated among lead firms in advanced economies, while weak backward and forward linkages constrain knowledge diffusion and functional upgrading, particularly for SMEs. Although these structural challenges are shared, they manifest differently depending on GVC governance. In buyer-driven chains such as coffee and T&C, asymmetric bargaining power between global buyers and local producers reinforces unequal value capture and weakens local investment incentives. In contrast, the producer-driven automotive sector offers greater upgrading potential but is characterised by modular production systems and stringent standards that limit technological learning and isolate domestic firms from innovation ecosystems. Sector-specific social and sustainability challenges also persist, including rural livelihoods and climate vulnerability in coffee, labour and compliance pressures in T&C, and skills and technological gaps in automobiles.

The Element further highlights emerging external risks to ASEAN's GVC-led development model. The resurgence of United States protectionism, particularly the enforcement of reciprocal tariff measures in 2025, poses significant challenges for highly trade-dependent economies. Tariff escalation has weakened export competitiveness, raised compliance costs, and reduced investment certainty, while delivering only limited and temporary trade diversion gains. Export-oriented sectors such as electronics, apparel, and motor vehicles are especially vulnerable, with SMEs and women workers disproportionately affected due to their concentration in labour-intensive and upstream segments of GVCs.

To transform GVC participation into a driver of resilient and inclusive development, the Element calls for a strategic shift from low-cost participation to active upgrading. Key policy directions include strengthening domestic innovation systems; supporting functional, process, and product upgrading; empowering SMEs through finance, skills, and standards compliance; and leveraging digitalisation to enhance firm capabilities and GVC participation. Public research institutes can play a critical intermediary role by helping firms identify, assess, and adapt imported technologies. At the regional level, deeper cooperation – through stronger RVCs, harmonised standards, and shared innovation platforms – can reduce vulnerability to external shocks. Finally, economic upgrading must be complemented by social and environmental upgrading, embedding labour rights, gender equality, and sustainability into industrial strategies.

This Element argues that while GVCs have been powerful engines of growth for ASEAN, they have also entrenched structural vulnerabilities that constrain long-term development. ASEAN's future transformation will depend on its ability to move from passive integration toward coordinated, capability-driven, and regionally anchored strategies that balance global competitiveness with inclusive and sustainable development outcomes.

[illegible]

Cambridge Elements

International Economics

Kenneth A. Reinert
George Mason University

Kenneth A. Reinert is Professor of Public Policy in the Schar School of Policy and Government at George Mason University where he directs the Global Commerce and Policy master's degree program. He is author of *An Introduction to International Economics: New Perspectives on the World Economy* with Cambridge University Press and coauthor of *Globalization for Development: Meeting New Challenges* with Oxford University Press. He is also editor of *The Handbook of Globalisation and Development* with Edward Elgar and co-editor of the two-volume *Princeton Encyclopedia of the World Economy* with Princeton University Press.

About the Series

International economics is a distinct field with both fundamental theoretical insights and increasing empirical and policy relevance. The *Cambridge Elements in International Economics* showcases this field, covering the subfields of international trade, international money and finance, and international production, and featuring both established researchers and new contributors from all parts of the world. It aims for a level of theoretical discourse slightly above that of the *Journal of Economic Perspectives* to maintain accessibility. It extends Cambridge University Press' established reputation in international economics into the new, digital format of *Cambridge Elements*. It attempts to fill the niche once occupied by the *Princeton Essays in International Finance*, a series that no longer exists.

There is a great deal of important work that takes place in international economics that is set out in highly theoretical and mathematical terms. This new Elements does not eschew this work but seeks a broader audience that includes academic economists and researchers, including those working in international organizations, such as the World Bank, the International Monetary Fund, and the Organization for Economic Cooperation and Development.

Cambridge Elements

International Economics

Elements in the Series

A full series listing is available at: www.cambridge.org/CEIE

Printed in the United Kingdom by TJ Clays Ltd.